In the name of Allah
The Merciful, the Compassionate

For

....

....

GOODWORD BOOKS

- The Qur'an
- Qur'an: An Abiding Wonder
- The Call of the Qur'an
- The Koran
- Heart of the Koran
- The Soul of the Qur'an
- Presenting the Qur'an
- The Moral Values of the Qur'an
- The Basic Concepts in the Qur'an
- A Treasury of the Qur'an
- The Qur'an for All Humanity
- The Beautiful Commands of Allah
- The Beautiful Promises of Allah
- The Wonderful Universe of Allah
- Muhammad: A Prophet for All Humanity
- Muhammad: A Mercy to All the Nations
- Words of the Prophet Muhammad
- The Sayings of Muhammad
- The Life of the Prophet Muhammad
- Muhammad: The Hero as Prophet
- History of the Prophet Muhammad
- An Islamic Treasury of Virtues
- A-Z Steps to Leadership
- Islam and Peace
- Introducing Islam
- The Moral Vision
- Tell Me About Hajj

- Principles of Islam
- The Muslim Prayer Encyclopaedia
- After Death, Life!
- Living Islam: Treading the Path of the Ideal
- A Basic Dictionary of Islam
- The Muslim Marriage Guide
- Essential Arabic
- Indian Muslims
- God Arises
- Islam: The Voice of Human Nature
- Islam: Creator of the Modern Age
- Woman Between Islam and Western Society
- Woman in Islamic Shari'ah
- Islam As It Is
- Religion And Science
- Man Know Thyself
- Muhammad: The Ideal Character
- Tabligh Movement
- Polygamy and Islam
- Hijab in Islam
- Concerning Divorce
- The Way to Find God
- The Teachings of Islam
- The Good Life
- The Garden of Paradise
- The Fire of Hell
- Islam and the Modern Man
- Uniform Civil Code

A Simple Guide To
Muslim Prayers

Shaikh Muhammad Mahmud Al-Sawwaf

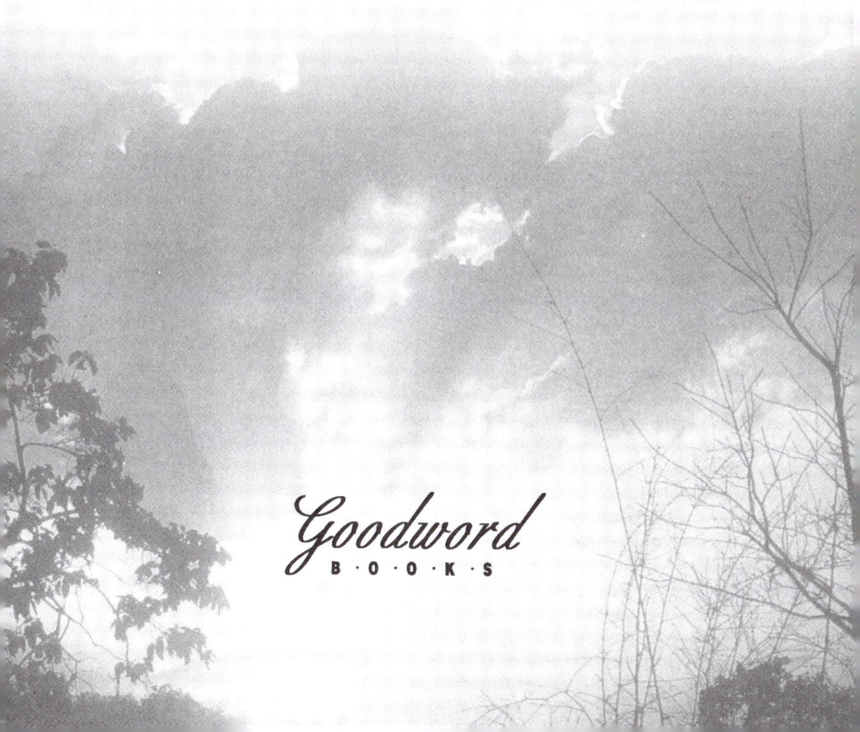

Goodword
B·O·O·K·S

© Goodword Books 2002
First published 2001, 2002

ISBN 81-87570-25-3

GOODWORD BOOKS
1, Nizamuddin West Market
New Delhi 110 013
Tel. 435 5454, 435 6666, 435 1128
Fax 435 7333, 435 7980
E-mail: info@goodwordbooks.com
Website: www.goodwordbooks.com

Contents

Introduction • 10

1 The Place of Prayer in Islam

1. Prayer, the pillar of religion • 13
2. The spiritual influence of prayer • 15
3. Prayer as a remedy for the heart • 16
4. Unity and equality in prayer • 18
5. The judgment on one who renounces prayer • 19
6. Expectation of the mercy of Allah • 27
7. Rejected prayer • 30
8. A weak argument • 32

2 Preparation for the Prayer

1. The meaning of prayer • 37
2. Preparation for prayer • 41
   - A - Cleanliness • 42
     1. General • 42
     2. Cleansing the body of impurity • 44
     3. How to perform the ritual ablution • 45
     4. Wiping the socks • 47

5 Things which invalidate the ablution • 47
6 Total ablution • 51
7 What necessitates total ablution • 51
8 How to carry out total ablution • 52
9 Purification with earth,
    A description of the purification • 53
10 Removing dirt • 60

B - The times of prayer • 61

1 General • 61
   a. The Morning prayer • 61
   b. The Noon prayer • 62
   c. The Afternoon prayer • 62
   d. The Sunset prayer • 63
   e. The Evening prayer • 63
2 The call to prayer • 64
3 A description of the call to prayer • 67
4 The second call (iqama) • 71

   Notes: • 74

C - Facing the direction of the Ka'bah • 76
1 General • 76
2 The rule when the direction of the Ka'bah
   cannot be determined • 77
3 When the direction of the Ka'bah is not faced • 79

3 How the prayer is performed

1. General • 83
2. The five prayers • 97
3. The voluntary prayers • 97
4. The Morning prayer • 98
   a. General • 98
   b. How the two *rak'as* are performed • 99
5. The Noon prayer (*zuhr*) • 111
   a. General • 111
   b. How to perform the four rak'as • 112
   c. Important note • 113
6. The Afternoon prayer (*'asr*) • 113
7. The Sunset prayer (*maghrib*) • 114
8. The Evening prayer (*'isha*) • 116
9. The witr prayer • 116
10. Some important notes • 122
11. The prostration of forgetfulness • 126
12. Performance of the prayer by one who is sick • 128
13. Congregational prayer • 129
14. How the congregational prayer is performed • 132
15. Prayer during a jouney • 136
16. Joining prayers together • 141
17. The Friday prayer • 143
    a. General • 143
    b. How to perform the Friday prayer • 146
18. The Prayer of the Two Feasts • 149
    a. The Prayer of the Feast of the Breaking of the Fast (*'Id-al-Fitr*) • 149

  b. The Prayer of the Feast of
   Sacrifice (*'Id-al-Adha*) • 153
  Important notes • 153
19. The Funeral prayer (*janaza*) • 154
  a. The first 'Words of Greatness' • 155
  b. The second 'Words of Greatness' • 157
  c. The third 'Words of Greatness' • 158
  d. The fourth 'Words of Greatness' • 158
20. The prayer for Allah's Guidance (*istikhara*) • 160
21. The prayer for the Eclipse of the Moon and
  the Eclipse of the Sun • 162
  a. The reason for the prayer for the Eclipse • 163
  b. How to perform the prayer of the Eclipse • 164
  c. Charity and forgiveness • 167
22. Conclusion • 169

Introduction

Praise be to the Compassionate and Merciful Allah, Just and Wise, Who grants His favour and mercy to whoever obeys Him, who is angered by and punishes whoever disobeys Him. He is Self-sufficient, All-powerful, the Greatest, the Most High. Praise be to him, Exalted be His Countenance, Mighty be His Dominion. It is He who judges, and it is to Him that we return.

I bear witness that there is no deity save Allah. It is He who has charged Muslims with the duty of saying five prayers daily and enjoined them from above the Seven Heavens to attend to their prayers, saying:

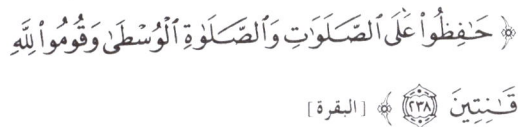

Say your prayers regularly, especially the Middle prayers, and stand before Allah with all devotion.

(*Surah al-Baqarah*, The Heifer, 2:238)

I bear witness that Muhammad is the Messenger of Allah, the most excellent of worshippers, leader of the God-fearing, Supreme among Prophets.

Sensing a praiseworthy inclination among many men, women and young people towards the true religion and everlasting message of Allah, I felt inspired to fulfil their urgent need for guidance by writing the present book of instructions on prayer.

They long to return to Allah and have an inner need to perform their religious duties, particularly that of prayer—that pillar of Islam which Allah has made the cornerstone of His religion and a beacon to the God-fearing. But they are hindered by their ignorance of the proper manner in which to perform them. This shortcoming is a cardinal sin against which all individuals should be on their guard. I mention this with utmost sorrow, having myself suffered along with many in this distressing situation. Most people are ashamed to let this inadequacy be known, for it is galling to have to admit that one has grown old and knowledgeable and achieved an enviable stature in society, without being able to say a simple prayer—something which even Muslim children should with confidence be able to do. Myriad souls are thus wasting away from the grief that springs from unsaid prayers, for by neglecting this great spiritual support, they are, in effect, cutting themselves off from Allah.

It was the urge to help others to fill this great gap in their lives which prompted me to write this book.

Since every Muslim needs to know the five prayers—the Friday prayer, the Congregational prayer, the prayer of the two Feasts, the prayer for the dead, the prayer during a journey and the prayer for Allah's guidance—I have included all of them. I have tried to use the simplest terms so that all, the young and the old, the educated and the uneducated alike will understand. Those who do already pray may benefit by having possible mistakes corrected, while those who do not as yet pray will find it easy to learn the prayers as set forth here. As far as possible, I have avoided contentious matters and have included only what has been established as having been correctly passed down from the Prophet and given the seal of approval by most of the Imams.

I beseech Allah's guidance in this work, for only He can assist me in this. I beseech Him to let my words convey their sincere intentions and to counsel my critics to pardon any errors they may find in it. May Allah grant me success in this. I ask Allah to grant that all readers may benefit from this, to forgive us our sins, our mistakes and our excesses, to guide our feet to the true path, to make us steadfast in our promise to our Lord, both in this world and on the Day of Resurrection. Allah is my all, the perfect Counsellor, the perfect Master, the perfect Helper.

Muhammad Mahmud Al-Sawwaf

One

The Place of Prayer in Islam

PRAYER, THE PILLAR OF RELIGION:

Every Muslim will testify to prayer being the cornerstone of religion, for he knows in his heart that it is the most important pillar of the faith. Indeed, it is this factor which divides Islam from non-Islam. As such it is of Supreme value to Allah.

The Prophet said that on the Day of Judgement the first thing that the servant of Allah would be called to account for would be prayer. If he had prayed sedulously and in the true spirit of piety, then his deeds must have been good; if not, his deeds must have been bad.[1]

WORSHIP OF GOD

Worship, in form, consists of the performance of certain ritual actions. In essence, it is to form a central focus. From this point of view everyone is worshipping something or the other. It is a rare being who does not cherish some overriding ambition, which he will do his utmost to realize. All men feel some insufficiency in themselves and need some help from outside to make up for it. When one yearns for God alone and puts implicit trust in Him, one is, in reality, worshipping Him. To concentrate one's emotions on something else is to worship others besides Him.

A person who worships God will invoke Him alone, and the prescribed prayers are the day-to-day form which this supplication will take. The worshipper becomes so involved with His Lord that his requirements become minimal; a particular form that this diminution takes is fasting. His adoration of God compels him to strive towards God, and one historic manifestation of his longing is Hajj. He does unto others as he would be done by, and in *zakat*—charity—this takes a regular, practical form.

The whole life of a true worshipper of God, both inwardly and outwardly, becomes an act of worship, bowing only to God and fearing Him alone—putting His considerations first and foremost in all matters. Placing oneself totally in God's hands, one becomes God's own, and God becomes one's own. And one's heart overflows with the love of God.

— *Introducing Islam* by Maulana Wahiduddin Khan

Indeed, Allah has made prayer the way to success, prosperity, and happiness:

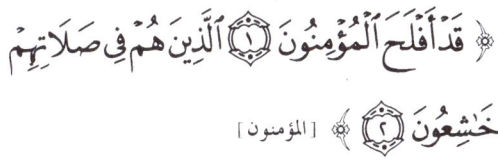

These believers who are humble in their prayers must (eventually) be prosperous.
(*Surah Al-Mu'minun*, The Believers, 23:1-2).

THE SPIRITUAL INFLUENCE OF PRAYER

Genuine prayer, based on humility and submission, illuminates the heart, purifies the soul, and teaches the worshipper both the refinements of worship and his obligations to the divinity of the great and Almighty Allah, for it is through prayer that the glory and majesty of Allah are implanted in his heart. Prayer endows man with such excellent virtues as truthfulness, honesty, moderation, integrity, understanding, modesty, fairness, and generosity.

It raises him up and directs him to the One God, increasing his fear and dread of Him. In this way, his moral standards are raised, his soul is purified, and he abstains from lying, falsehood, evil, deception, anger and pride, and is then able to rise above injustice, enmity, meanness, iniquity and disobedience. Thus he proves the word of the Qur'an to be true:

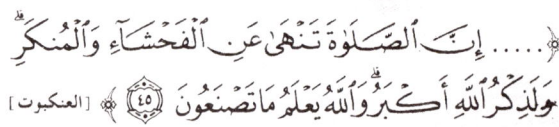

Prayer restrains man from indecency and evil. And remembrance of Allah is the greatest thing in life. And Allah knows the deeds that you do.

(*Surah Al-'Ankabut,* The Spider, 29:45)

PRAYER AS A REMEDY FOR THE HEART

Prayer has a form and a spirit. Its form is worship with the body, while its spirit is worship with the heart. It is both a material and a spiritual exercise. The heart and countenance of one who performs it will shine with divine light, and his soul will be uplifted. It is the link between the slave and his Master.

The performance of prayers is one of the greatest tokens of faith, the most significant of religious ceremonies, and the surest way of thanking Allah for His boundless favours. To neglect it is to be separated from Allah. It is to be deprived of His mercy, the abundance of His favours, and the plenitude of His generosity. It is to be refused of His kindness and blessings.

Earnest prayer is the remedy for the ills which beset the heart and corrupt the soul. It is the light which dispels the darkness of evil and sin. According to Abu Hurayra, the Prophet said, "Look, if any one of you had a river at his door and bathed in it five times a day, would any of his dirt be left?" They replied, "None of his dirt would be left." He said, "This is like the five prayers by which Allah washes away our sins."[2]

UNITY AND EQUALITY IN PRAYER

Equality and justice are made manifest through prayers. When the *muezzin* calls: "Come to prayers, come to prosperity," all those whose duty it is to pray and who hear his call, be they rich or poor, young or old, ruler or subject, despite the differences between them they become equals—all of them are servants of Allah. In the house of Allah, they meet on common ground, thinking only of Him and humbling themselves before Him.

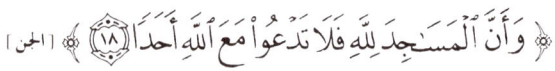

And the places of worship are for Allah (alone); therefore invoke no other along with Allah.

(*Al-Jinn*, The Jinn, 72:18)

Standing behind one Imam, they face in one direction, worship One God who has no partner, and become humble and submissive, fearing His punishment and craving His mercy. Assuredly, divine blessings will descend upon them and they will be encompassed by His mercy.

﴿ وَٱدْعُوهُ خَوْفًا وَطَمَعًا إِنَّ رَحْمَتَ ٱللَّهِ قَرِيبٌ مِّنَ ٱلْمُحْسِنِينَ ۝ ﴾ [الأعراف]

Pray to Him with fear and longing (in your heart): for the Mercy of Allah is near to those who do good.

(*Al-'Araf*, The Heights, 7:56)

THE JUDGMENT ON ONE WHO RENOUNCES PRAYERS

Allah has ordained prayer and made it the beacon of Islam and the pillar of the religion. The Prophet said, "On top is Islam. The pillar which supports it is Prayer and the highest place in it is the struggle for the cause of Allah."[3]

Prayer, the first of the religious observances decreed by Allah, it was ordained on the night of the Prophet's ascension to the seven heavens. Because of its importance and the great value which Allah places upon it, He spoke directly to His Messenger, with no intermediary. For this reason He severely reproaches all those who desist from it, considering them to be non-believers and to have strayed from the true path.

He who turns away from prayers turns away from Islam and angers his Lord. He breaks the commandments of his faith and sets himself on the road to ruin. In so doing he renders all his good deeds useless, for he acts contrary to the Allah's pronouncements on prayer—and one who disobeys Allah is virtually one who denies Him, for were he to acknowledge Allah's words, surely he would have obeyed this, the most divine of all commands.

Alminghty Allah has said:

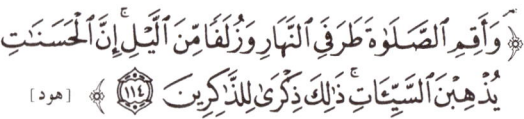

Attend to your prayers morning and evening and at the approach of night, for good deeds shall make amends for sins. That is an admonition for thoughtful people.

(Surah Hud, 11:114)

﴿ ..... وَأَقِمِ ٱلصَّلَوٰةَ إِنَّ ٱلصَّلَوٰةَ تَنْهَىٰ عَنِ ٱلْفَحْشَاءِ وَٱلْمُنكَرِ ..... ۝ ﴾ [العنكبوت]

Say regular prayers. Prayer restrains man from indecency and evil.

(Surah al-'Ankabut, The Spider, 29:45)

﴿ فَإِذَا ٱطْمَأْنَنتُمْ فَأَقِيمُوا۟ ٱلصَّلَوٰةَ ۚ إِنَّ ٱلصَّلَوٰةَ كَانَتْ عَلَى ٱلْمُؤْمِنِينَ كِتَٰبًا مَّوْقُوتًا ۝ ﴾ [النساء]

But when you are free from danger attend to your prayers regularly, for such prayers are enjoined on believers at stated times.

(Surah an-Nisa', Women, 4:103)

The Prophet said: "What divides a perfect man from an unbeliever is the renouncing of prayers."[4]

According to Burayda the Prophet said, "The obligation which separates us from them is prayer. He who renounces it has become an unbeliever."[5]

Abd Allah Ibn Amr relates that one day, speaking of prayers, the Prophet said, "For one who observes it, it becomes a light, a proof and a deliverance on the Day of Judgment. For one who does not observe it, there is no light, no proof, no deliverance, and on the Day of Judgment he will be like Qarun, Fir'awn (Pharaoh) and Ubayy Ibn Khalaf."[6]

These honoured Traditions of the Prophet and the commands in the Qur'an clearly show the enormity of the sin of one who renounces prayers. They also indicate what his place will be in this world and in the Hereafter.

Given these and other Traditions, and because of the importance of prayer in Islam, certain of the Companions and many of their learned contemporaries held that whoever renounced prayer become a non-believer. In their view, even one who renounced prayer without abandoning his basic belief in its religious merit, had nevertheless strayed from the true path and ought to be punished by an Islamic authority until he returned to it. He would not then set others a bad example.

Among those who believed that such a person must be punished were Malik, Al-Shafi'i, and Abu Hanifa and his followers.[7]

Thus the Law of Islam severely admonishes its members and requires of them sincere adherence to Islamic law through the continuous practice of prayers, the most important pillar of Islam and the greatest of religious duties. No wonder then that we hear one who neglects his prayers adjudged as a nonbeliever or as one who has strayed from the truth, for we read in the Qur'an and we see that he who abandons prayers is called an evil-doer and is numbered among the sinners who will go down to Hell:

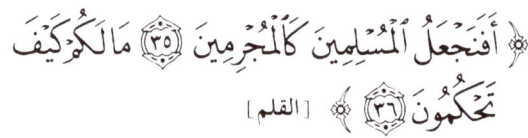

Shall we then treat the believers the same as the sinners? What is the matter with you that you should judge so ill?
(*Surah al-Qalam,* The Pen, 68:35-36)

Indeed, the Qur'an further explains and describes the wrong-doer who encounters the believer, saying:

﴿ كُلُّ نَفْسٍ بِمَا كَسَبَتْ رَهِينَةٌ ۝ إِلَّا أَصْحَابَ ٱلْيَمِينِ ۝ فِي جَنَّاتٍ يَتَسَاءَلُونَ ۝ عَنِ ٱلْمُجْرِمِينَ ۝ مَا سَلَكَكُمْ فِي سَقَرَ ۝ قَالُوا لَمْ نَكُ مِنَ ٱلْمُصَلِّينَ ۝ وَلَمْ نَكُ نُطْعِمُ ٱلْمِسْكِينَ ۝ وَكُنَّا نَخُوضُ مَعَ ٱلْخَائِضِينَ ۝ وَكُنَّا نُكَذِّبُ بِيَوْمِ ٱلدِّينِ ۝ حَتَّىٰ أَتَانَا ٱلْيَقِينُ ۝ فَمَا تَنفَعُهُمْ شَفَاعَةُ ٱلشَّافِعِينَ ۝ ﴾ [المدثر]

Every soul will be held in pledge for its deeds. Except the Companions of the right hand. They will reside in Gardens of Delight: they will question the sinners about what led them into Hell. The latter will say, "We never prayed; nor did we ever feed the indigent, but we used to engage in vain disputes; and we used to deny the Day of Judgment until Death overtook us. No intercessor's plea shall save them.

(*Surah al-Muddaththir*, The One Wrapped Up, 74: 38-48)

To abandon prayers then is to follow the road to Hell which leaves nothing, spares nothing, and consumes men with its heat—a proper reward. This judgment is not excessive for one who has violated the teaching of the Prophet—whom Allah has sent as His Messenger and guide to mankind—who having heard and understood the words of Allah setting limits to his actions, has resisted and disobeyed them, who, in short, has been too proud to worship his Lord. If he pauses to consider for only a moment, he will surely realize that by abandoning prayers he has put himself outside the pale of Islam and that he has no right to protest against this righteous judgment, especially after reading its description in the Qur'an and the Traditions of the Prophet.

The mere fact of being linked with something does not entitle one to expect any benefit from it if one's deeds do not befit the association. Let us have some examples: Suppose you have been engaged to work in an office. When are you entitled to be called an employee and take your salary?

Don't you actually have to do your work? And doesn't the head of your office record the date you begin? Don't you keep office hours and work until the end of the month to receive your salary? If you fail to do the prescribed work, or to apply yourself to the task until its completion, will the office put up with you patiently? Will they pay you? Of course not! Even if a formal order has been issued for your appointment, it is still quite easy to cancel it and dismiss you.

You belong to some institute or school. Aren't you required to attend class regularly and do all the staff asks of you? If you disobey the staff and ignore their instructions, if you break the rules and regulations of the school or institute, will you continue to be a member of it, or will you be expelled? There is no doubt that you would be dismissed and your membership of the institution would become null and void.

THOSE WHO BOW BEFORE GOD

God requires for paradise realistic souls who live as if they are seeing God, though He is invisible; who are so conscious of God's greatness and perfection that He is always in their thoughts. Their lives should be so centred on God that their hearts should pulsate to His words.

The wondrous world of paradise will be inhabited by those who are so devoted to God that He comes to dominate their lives; who raise their consciousness to a level which enables them to look at themselves objectively; who, although they are free, place constraints upon themselves and practise self-discipline.

When one reaches this stage of high-mindedness and realism, one develops objectivity in one's thinking; one begins to see oneself in a true rather than a personal light; one submits totally to the Creator, though one is not forced to do so; one keeps to God's commandments, even in the face of temptation; one accepts truth fully, even though one is in a position to reject it; one has the same attitude of submission to the Lord of Creation now, when He is invisible, as one will have when He becomes visible in the hereafter.

— *Introducing Islam* by Maulana Wahiduddin Khan

If you join the army, either as an officer or as a private soldier, aren't you required to wear a uniform? Don't you attend to the orders of your superiors and obey them without question or delay? If you refused to wear the uniform, or if after having put it on, you flout your superiors' commands and military regulations, thus failing in all the obligations of this respected calling, do you think you would be allowed to remain in service? Don't you think you would be discharged without delay as being unfit for this honourable profession, thus losing all your privileges?

Islam operates in a similar fashion. You accept Allah as your Master, Islam as your religion, and Muhammad (peace be upon him) as your Prophet and Messenger. Are you not required then to carry out the obligations of the religion, to perform all religious duties, and to support its first principles? Is it not necessary, to be an adherent, to carry out the most important of its commands—the obligation to perform the prayers? This is the distinguishing mark of the Muslim, just as the uniform is the distinguishing mark of the soldier. Are you not required to heed the commands of the Qur'an, which was revealed by the Lord Almighty and to comply with every single order, if you are to be associated with the Qur'an and its community? Are you not required to be guided by your Prophet, to follow his light, and to meet his every wish, seeing that he has commanded you to obey him and follow in his footsteps? If you ignore the commands of your Lord and the instructions of your Prophet, if you put the Qur'an behind you and demolish the buttresses of Islam one by one, until finally prayer itself is torn down, do you think that, having done so, you are still entitled to call yourself a Muslim? Should the mere fact of your connection with Islam be of any advantage to you? Shouldn't you be deprived of it? You will certainly be expelled, and barriers will be erected between it and you. This answer is in my opinion, according to the Law, and—as you must see yourself—it is patently clear and generally recoganised.

The Prophet said, "What lies between a perfect man and the unbeliever is the renouncing of prayer."[8] The unbelievers are the ones who suffer.

EXPECTATION OF THE MERCY OF ALLAH

Because of your belief that Almighty Allah is Omnipotent, abounding in forgiveness and pardon, and ever near in His mercy, you should not think that religion is inconsistent with the examples I have given you. The reason is that His mercy is all-embracing and closest of all to man, especially to one who believes in Him:

For the Mercy of Allah is near those who do good.

(*Surah al-A'raf,* The Heights, 7:56).

$$\text{﴿ وَرَحْمَتِى وَسِعَتْ كُلَّ شَىْءٍ فَسَأَكْتُبُهَا لِلَّذِينَ يَتَّقُونَ وَيُؤْتُونَ ٱلزَّكَوٰةَ وَٱلَّذِينَ هُم بِـَٔايَـٰتِنَا يُؤْمِنُونَ ﴾ [الأعراف]}$$

My mercy extends to all things. That [mercy] I shall ordain for those who do right and practice regular charity and those who believe in Our signs.

(*Surah al-A'raf,* The Heights, 7: 156).

In one of the holy Traditions (*hadith qudsi*), the Prophet called to mind that Allah had said:

"How impudent is he who aspires to My Garden without working for it. How can I pour My mercy on one who refuses to obey Me?"

Mercy is obtained by good deeds, piety, alms giving, and reverence for Allah. Faith is proved by the actions which spring from that faith. Faith does not come simply by wishing for it, but from resolution and steadfastness in the soul and from the deeds which attest to it.

Al-Bukhari relates[9] a tradition of Anas ibn Malik which is traceable to the Prophet:

"Faith is not wishing but is what is implanted in the soul and attested to by deeds. Wishes mislead people, so that they leave this life without having performed a single good deed. They say, 'We reverenced Allah', but they lie. Had they felt reverence, they would have done good deeds."

I hope after this that you have not despaired of the mercy of Allah, for it is close to you, ready to be taken. Turn to Allah in repentance and be of the worshippers who prostrate themselves, obtaining the mercy, forgiveness, and favour of Allah which your soul desires. Here lie prosperity and happiness in this world and the next.

Hasten to repent. The door of repentance is always open for those who would enter. Draw close to Allah and Allah will draw close to you; no one can grant you greater help. Perform your religious duties and present yourself to Allah with humility, with worship, and prostration. Allah will forgive your sins, pardon your misdeeds, and grant you His mercy. He will give you gardens and palaces. Hasten to true prayer which keeps you away from evil and what is forbidden, for this will bring you close to Allah.

But this will be impossible unless the prayer is humble and sincere before Allah, Lord of Heaven and Earth. If it is tainted by hypocrisy, the labours of the one who performs it will be rendered worthless and futile.

REJECTED PRAYER

The fundamental point about prayer is that it purifies the soul, refines the character, and keeps the one who performs it from falsehood and all forbidden actions. It cleanses one of baseness and shamefulness. One who prays, yet at the same time misappropriates others' possessions, who spreads evil among men, and whose actions belie the noble precepts of religion, who, perhaps, prays only to have people's good opinion, or simply uses prayer as a screen for his many misdeeds, will find that the benefits which his prayers should bring him, and which should restrain him from doing evil, will be cancelled out.

We may take it for granted that one who so misuses prayer, will have his prayers rejected as futile. They will be rolled up like a bundle of worn-out cloths and thrown in his face, whether he likes it or not. His prayers will avail him nothing and will not draw him near to Allah. Rather, it will increase his distance from Him and incur more loss on his part, for a Tradition of the Prophet says, "He whose prayers have not restrained him from evil and misdeeds has only increased his distance from Allah."[10]

Furthermore, the Law of Islam rejects the prayer of one who does not persevere in it, who neither performs the ritual ablution properly, nor prays with humility, nor bows the body, nor prostrates himself, for inattention to these matters shows a lack of interest in them. If one ignores these important first principles, then why should one concern oneself with what follows them?

In the Tradition related by Anas ibn Malik the Prophet said:

"One who has performed the prayers at the right times, who has carried out its ritual ablutions, and the requirements of standing, submission, bowing and prostration, shall see his prayers emerge shining white. It will say, 'May Allah protect you as you have protected me.' But one who has performed the prayer at other than the right times, who has not carried out its ritual ablutions, or the requirements of submission, bowing, and prostration, shall see his prayer emerge the darkest black. It will say, 'May Allah ruin you as you have ruined me.' So when it arrives where it is intended, it will be rolled up like a bundle of old clothes, then he will be struck with it on the face."[11]

Listen to the words of the Almighty, as related in the holy tradition (*Hadith Qudsi*), which explains from whom prayers will be accepted. Let this be a warning to those of you who have strayed from the path and those who have adopted religion as a means of achieving their private ends, who pray only for their own requirements. May Allah turn against them while they are so alienated and let them see what Allah promises to those whose prayers are accepted.

According to the Prophet, Almighty Allah said: "I will accept the prayer of one who humbles himself before My Greatness, who does not display arrogance towards what I create, who does not constantly spend the night disobeying Me, who spends the day remembering Me, who has compassion for the wretched, the wayfarer the widow, and the afflicted. That man's light is like the light of the sun. I will protect him with My might, guard him with My angels, be a light for him in the darkness, in ignorance and understanding." His likeness in my creatures is as Paradise in the gardens."[12]

These Traditions make clear the judgment on those who mix good deeds with bad. Can this possibly be advanced as an argument by those who would use it as evidence by which to discredit religion and prayers—unjustly and with enmity?

A WEAK ARGUMENT

Some people, when I have urged them to perform the prayers, have replied: "Religion lies not only in prayers. There are many who pray, yet their hearts are wicked, and their actions apart from prayers are evil. As for us, our hearts are pure... we love religion and we respect it more than many who pray" and so on. Their argument is weak.

They are under the impression that the actions and prayers of these people which will be cast back into their faces are an argument against religion and prayers per se. They think that religion should become a tomb which exists only in the heart and should have no outward sign which would demonstrate "if nothing else" the conviction of the heart and the life of this religion.

Fear Allah! Try to find favour with Him! Hasten to do good works before you are distracted! Forge a link between yourself and your Lord with much prayer and alms-giving, and with many good deeds!

Know that Islam is not prayer alone, nor only a pure heart. No! It is prayer and purity, love and loyalty; it is steadfastness, good deeds, and hospitality; it is pilgrimage and bearing witness; it is alms-giving and worshipping; it is struggle for the cause of Allah and sincere devotion to Him.

Call upon Him, giving Him sincere devotion and none besides Him.

(*Surah al-Mu'min*, The Believer, 40:14)

Guidance and worship; faith, knowledge and endeavour; wisdom and dignity; paradise and hell; obedience and reverence; a community and an organized society.

Islam, a coherent unit, is indivisible. It is not possible to believe one part of the Book and disbelieve another part. It must be accepted in its entirety. Working to achieve this faith means working at all of it.

A believer should fear Allah and turn to Him before death overtakes him, for whoever turns to Him, to him He turns, forgiving him and granting him His favour. The mercy of Allah is more liberal than that bestowed on one who approaches Him in search of it. Acknowledge Allah in times of prosperity and He will acknowledge you in times of adversity. Turn back to your religion and thrive, seek the help of Allah. Recite the Qur'an and understand it. It will be for you a treasure and a light. Follow the light which Prophet Muhammad (peace be upon him) brought to you. Seek the Hereafter through what Allah has given you, but do not forget your part in this world, transient though it may be, and even though it be filled with pleasure and amusement.

Do good and Allah will do good to you. Do not seek the wickedness of the world. Say your prayers and give alms. Bow down with those who bow down.

Fight for Allah in His holy war. A great struggle awaits you.

If we do not offer Allah pious deeds by patience, and preparation, ill fortune will befall us and, Allah forbid, we shall become the losers. Therefore, fear Allah.

﴿ وَسَارِعُوٓا۟ إِلَىٰ مَغْفِرَةٍ مِّن رَّبِّكُمْ وَجَنَّةٍ عَرْضُهَا ٱلسَّمَـٰوَٰتُ وَٱلْأَرْضُ أُعِدَّتْ لِلْمُتَّقِينَ ۝١٣٣ ٱلَّذِينَ يُنفِقُونَ فِى ٱلسَّرَّآءِ وَٱلضَّرَّآءِ وَٱلْكَـٰظِمِينَ ٱلْغَيْظَ وَٱلْعَافِينَ عَنِ ٱلنَّاسِ وَٱللَّهُ يُحِبُّ ٱلْمُحْسِنِينَ ۝١٣٤ ﴾ [آل عمران]

Be quick in the race for your Lord's forgiveness, for a garden whose width is that of all the heavens and the earth is prepared for the righteous: those who give alms, whether in prosperity or in adversity, who restrain anger and pardon their fellow men, because Allah loves those who do good.

(*Surah al-'Imran*, The Family of 'Imran, 3:133-134)

May Allah direct us to the true path, reconcile us to obedience, delight us through prayers, afford us all help, give back the glory to religion Islam, predispose to this religion those who would protect it. Almighty Allah is the greatest Protector, the greatest of Helpers. Praise be to Allah, Lord of heaven and earth.

Preparation for the Prayer

THE MEANING OF PRAYER

he meaning of the Arabic word for prayer (*salah*) is "supplication" or "request." The Arabic language has another word with the latter meaning but, because this word is used in a more general sense, a further word which would mean, specifically, the invocation of Allah had to be found. It is said that the word the Arabs now use originally meant "to glorify." Specific acts of devotion, therefore, are called prayer, because in them we glorify Allah, as Islam commands we should and as the Prophet Muhammad (peace be upon him), explained. The Companions, those who came after him, and the leaders of the religion, have followed him in this. The word has now come to have the following meaning:

The worship and glorification of Allah by specific words and actions, commencing with the words: "Allah is Great" (الله أكبر) and ending with the words: (السلام عليكم ورحمة الله وبركاته) "May peace and the mercy of Allah be with you." This is a specially ordered and regulated form which Islam has brought into being, and which all Muslims follow as a light and guide. The word nevertheless retains linguistic nuances of "supplication" and "glorification."

The meaning of our saying, "Prayers belong to Allah", (الصلوات لله) is that Allah and Allah alone is entitled to receive the supplications by which it is intended to glorify Him.

The meaning of our saying (اللهم صل على محمد) "O Lord, bless Muhammad"[13] is: "O Lord, glorify him in this life by exalting his memory, grant success to his mission, and preserve his Law." It means to ask for his intercession in the Hereafter on behalf of his community, and for a great reward for him because of his good deeds. It has been said that its meaning originated when Allah commanded us to pray for the Prophet, on whom He had bestowed His friendship, and because we were incapable of discharging that divine duty, we left it to God saying, "O Lord, bless Muhammad, for You know what befits him."

Ours is supplication and glorification. Almighty Allah has said:

﴿ إِنَّ ٱللَّهَ وَمَلَٰٓئِكَتَهُۥ يُصَلُّونَ عَلَى ٱلنَّبِىِّ يَٰٓأَيُّهَا ٱلَّذِينَ ءَامَنُوا۟ صَلُّوا۟ عَلَيْهِ وَسَلِّمُوا۟ تَسْلِيمًا ﴾ [الأحزاب]

Allah and his Angels give their blessings to the Prophet. O you who believe! Bless him and salute him with all respect.

(*Surah al-Ahzab*, The Confederates, 33:56)

Prayer is an individual duty incumbent on every Muslim man and woman over the age of puberty, who have heard the message of the Prophet Muhammad (peace be upon him), and being of sound mind, clean and undefiled, are capable of performing it. A child is required to perform the prayer from the age of seven, so that he or she will be brought up to love it and make a habit of it. If by the age of ten he has not yet developed the habit of prayer, he must then be constrained to perform this religious duty.

There are many verses in the Qur'an concerning prayers, the following being only a few of them:

﴿ إِنَّ ٱلصَّلَوٰةَ كَانَتْ عَلَى ٱلْمُؤْمِنِينَ كِتَٰبًا مَّوْقُوتًا ﴾ [النساء]

Prayer is enjoined on Believers at stated times to be conducted at appointed hours

(*Surah al-Nisa*, The Woman, 4:103)

GOD'S WORSHIPPERS

Only one who has really been in love with someone can be moved to tears by the memory of his beloved. If one feels no attachment for someone, one cannot, simply because some occasion calls for it, force oneself to cry for that person.

Some adopt an attitude of humility towards their fellow men, while others remain arrogant. Some are fair and just, others oppress and persecute their fellows. Some are humble, others are proud. Some submit to the truth, others do not. People of such opposing attitudes cannot both worship God in a similar fashion. Only the first category of people will be genuinely humble in their worship. The second category may adopt the humble postures of worship—as the occasion demands—but they cannot thereby become God's humble servants. Humility in one's worship stems from a life of humility. One who is not humble in the totality of his existence cannot then be truly humble in his worship.

Those who truly worship God will enter paradise. They are the ones who serve God at all times, not just at specified times of worship. Paradise is an abode of truth. It has been prepared specially for those who are true in their worship. Those who are insincere will never be admitted to such an abode.

— *Introducing Islam* by Maulana Wahiduddin Khan

﴿ وَأْمُرْ أَهْلَكَ بِالصَّلَوٰةِ وَاصْطَبِرْ عَلَيْهَا ۖ لَا نَسْـَٔلُكَ رِزْقًا ۖ نَّحْنُ نَرْزُقُكَ ۗ وَٱلْعَٰقِبَةُ لِلتَّقْوَىٰ ۝ ﴾ [طـه]

Enjoin prayer on your people and be constant in its observance. We do not ask you to provide sustenance: We provide it for you. But (the fruit of) the Hereafter is for righteousness.

(Surah Ta Ha, 20:132)

﴿ وَأَقِيمُوا۟ ٱلصَّلَوٰةَ وَءَاتُوا۟ ٱلزَّكَوٰةَ وَٱرْكَعُوا۟ مَعَ ٱلرَّٰكِعِينَ ۝ ﴾ [البقرة]

And be steadfast in prayers; practise regular charity, and bow down your heads[14] with those who bow down (in worship).

(Surah al-Baqarah, The Heifer, 2:43)

There are also many Traditions of the Prophet concerning the importance of prayer and the obligation to perform it. Among other things, they explain the qualities of prayer and the punishment awaiting those who renounce it.

PREPARATION FOR PRAYER

One is not permitted to perform the prayer without fulfilling certain conditions, which are as follows:

First: Cleanliness. This includes cleanliness of the body, the garments, and the place where prayers are performed.

Second: Modest attire. In the case of a man, it is preferable and prudent that he be in normal dress and should be covered at least from the navel to the knee. A woman's body should be totally covered except for her hands and face.

Third: Being punctual in starting the prayers.

Fourth: Facing the Ka'bah. This means facing towards the sacred house of Allah in Makkah.

Cleanliness

Islam appeared in the arid Arab Peninsula where cultivation is scanty because of a shortage of water. In spite of that, it brought with it proper standards of civilization, demanding complete cleanliness and adherance to the essential virtues. It established the bases of worship as:

a. Purifying the heart of the murk of doubt, polytheism, misgiving, deviation, hypocrisy, dissimulation, hatred, rancour, and envy. The Muslim has been instructed that Allah sees him and that nothing at all may be hidden from Him:

Allah knows the furitive look and all that the hearts conceal.

(Surah al-Mu'min, The Believer, 40:19)

b. Cleansing the body and purifying it of filth, dirt, and defilement. Almighty Allah has said:

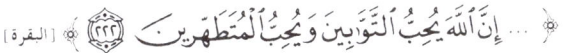

Allah loves those who turn to Him constantly and He loves those who keep themselves pure and clean.

(Surah al-Baqarah, The Heifer, 2:222)

The Prophet said: "Cleanliness is half of faith,"[15] and "The key to prayer is cleanliness. To say the Words of Greatness is to begin it, to say the Words of Peace is to finish it."[16]

A proverb says, "Cleanliness is a part of Faith."[17] This is the first condition for entering into prayer. As already stated, it includes cleanliness of the heart and body, of the garments, and of the place where the prayers are to be performed.

Cleansing the body of impurity

Impurity falls under two headings:

a. The Lesser Impurity. Caused by exertion or the passing of water or wind. This calls for ritual ablution or the substitute for it (When water is impossible to obtain or when there is good reason for water not to be used).

b. The Greater Impurity. The impurities which occasion the need for the washing of the entire body are intromission, ejaculation, menstruation and childbirth. The Qur'an says:

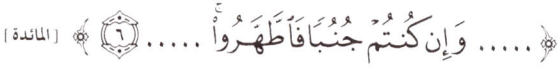

If you are in a state of impurity, cleanse yourselves.

(*Surah al-Ma'idah*, The Table Spread, 5:6).

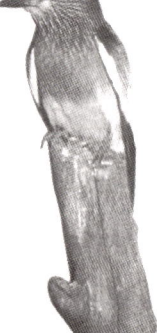

How to perform the ritual ablution

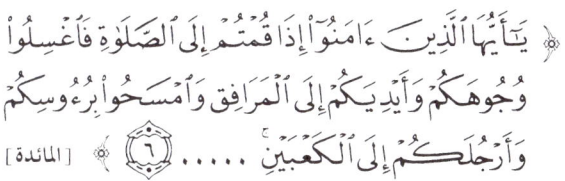

Almighty Allah has said:

Believers, when you prepare for prayer, wash your faces and your hands to the elbows, rub your heads and your feet to the ankles.

(*Surah al-Ma'idah*, The Table Spread, 5:6)

Because of this verse, ablution became a religious duty: without it prayer is not valid. It is not permissible to say prayers until the ablution has been carried out.

In resolving to begin the ritual ablution there is no requirement that the intention be spoken aloud or that any formality accompany it. On the contrary, it is sufficient that it is in your thoughts and that you are determined, in your heart, to carry out the ablution. Then pronounce the name of Allah by saying, "In the name of Allah, the Compassionate, the Merciful" and wash your hands to the wrist three times, passing the fingers of one hand between those of the other, and rubbing the hands well.

Next, take some water in your cupped hands and use it to rinse your mouth three times. Make an effort to use the *miswak*[18] to clean the teeth at the same time as rinsing the mouth. The traditional practice of using the *miswak* is fully authenticated.

Alternatively, rub your teeth with the thumb and forefinger. Many Traditions have come down regarding the *miswak*, among them being one in which the Prophet said:

"If it had not been too great a burden on my people, I would have bidden them to use the *miswak* at every prayer."[19]

Then the water is sniffed up the nostrils and blown out three times in order to clean the nose. After this, wash your face three times, making sure that the water reaches the creases of the face, the outside of the eyelids, and indeed the whole face. Then wash the arms to the elbows three times, the right arm before the left.

Next, take some water in your hands and sprinkle it over your head, wiping your head with your hands first from front to back and then from back to front. It is permissible to wipe part of the head with one hand only.

Next rub your ears inside and outside without taking fresh water (i.e. using the same water as you wiped your head with). Finally wash your feet three times down to the ankle, the right foot before the left.

Having finished the ablution, you may now recite the profession of Faith: "I bear witness that there is no deity save Allah: I bear witness that Muhammad is His Messenger."[20]

Continue, saying:

"O Lord, make me of those who turn to You in repentance and of those who are undefiled."[21]

It is essential that the ablution be carried out in the order mentioned above.

This then is the ritual ablution which will permit you to stand before your Lord and which will be valid for two or more times of prayers, provided that this state of cleanliness is maintained.

Wiping the socks

This is done according to the Tradition[22] of the Prophet. The top of the foot is wiped and not the sole, one day and night while at home. The traveller does this during the day and at night every three days. The feet must be cleaned before putting on footwear and it is permissible to wipe over woollen or other kinds of stockings.

This latter is a dispensation for the people.

Things which invalidate the ablution

The ablution is invalidated if any of the following occur, in which case it must be carried out anew:

a. The passing of excrement, urine, or wind. In the case of those who are afflicted with a condition of permanent wetting, their ablution is not rendered invalid even though this defilement occurs during prayers. In this case, they should carry out the ablution before every prayer.

b. Sleeping, no matter what the circumstances. However, if one is sitting down—as for instance in the mosque awaiting the prayers—and is overcome by drowsiness, in such a case the ablution is not invalidated.

c. Fainting, becoming unconscious, madness, drunkenness, and drug taking, etc., invalidate the ablution.

d. Touching the sexual organs intentionally and unclothed.

e. Vomiting.

PRAYERS OF THE PROPHET

Prophet Muhammad taught us that prayer is a way of saying how we need Allah's grace for every single thing we have, and how Allah's power over all things is total. There are different kinds of prayers. Some are to praise Allah for all the wonderful things in the world and some are to thank Him for His blessings. We often ask Allah to forgive us, telling Him of our fears and worries. At other times we pray for others to be helped and cared for.

The Prophet advised people to pray in times of peace and plenty, and not just in times of difficulty. One of his favourite prayers in the Qur'an was for parents: "My Lord, have mercy on them, as they have raised me up when I was little." He also said brotherly love was a great virtue. In his prayers to his Creator for all of humanity, he would say: "O Lord, all Your servants are brothers."

The Prophet urged his followers to ask Allah for forgiveness: "Allah holds out His hand at night for those who have done wrong during the day to repent. And He holds out His hand during the day for those who have done wrong at night to repent."

To have God's special protection, he would pray, "Allah, save me from leprosy, insanity and incurable diseases. O Allah, save me from want, poverty and being humbled. Save me from doing wrong or being wronged."

The Prophet forbade believers to pray for their own deaths or even to think about suicide. "If anyone is in a very dreadful state," said the Prophet, "let him pray, 'O Allah, keep me alive so long as life is good for me, and take away my soul to Yourself when death is best for me.' "

One who prays for another in his or her absence will most probably have his prayers fulfilled for, as the Prophet explained, to every believer Allah has assigned an angel who says, "Amen! And to you the same." His own selflessness is shown by his praying even for those who harmed him.

The Prophet, a keen observer of nature, regarded all natural things with a great sense of wonder. For example, seeing a new moon, he would pray, "O Allah, let its rays bring us security, peace and submission." Speaking to the moon, he would continue, "My Lord and Your Lord is Allah. May this be a crescent of guidance and goodness."

The Prophet would urge people to remember Allah constantly, as he believed that "one who remembers his Lord and one who does not remember his Lord are as unlike as the living and the dead." Therefore, the Prophet would urge his followers to remember Allah by day and by night, even if only by saying a few words. To make it easy for them to do this, he taught them a short prayer, saying:

Two phrases are light on the tongue yet heavy in the Balance and loved by the Merciful:

> *Subhan Allah wa bihamdihi,*
> *Subhan Allahil-Azeem.*

(Glory be to Allah and all Praises are His, Glory be to Allah, the Magnificent.)

— *Tell Me About the Prophet Muhammad* by Saniyasnain Khan

Note: If, knowing with certainty that you have performed the ablution, you entertain misgivings that you might have committed one of the above actions, but cannot be certain that you have done so, then your ablution is not invalidated, because doubt does not prevail over certainty.

Total ablution

Total ablution is cleaning the body with pure water, pouring it over the whole body and the hair of the head. A good healthy bath is also a pleasant way of cleaning the body, purifying it of the dirt which clings to it, and refreshing it.

What necessitates total ablution

Total ablution is obligatory in the following cases:

a. After the ejaculation of semen.

b. After sexual intercourse.

c. Following a dream, by a man or woman, of an erotic nature. Total ablution is obligatory if the dreamer finds any trace of semen on his clothes or bed. However, should he see in his dream that which would require his total ablution, yet on waking find no trace on his clothes or bed, then he is not required to carry out a total ablution. For a woman it is the same as for a man. If she should see any fluid, total ablution is obligatory, otherwise not. According to the Tradition, "fluid necessitates fluid."[23]

Equally, should a person on waking find the signs even though he has not a dream, he is required to perform total ablution.

d. Following menstruation a woman must carry out total ablution.

e. At the end of forty days after childbirth, a women is required to carry out total ablution. If, however, the haemorrhaging of childbirth ceases before forty days have passed, she may carry out total ablution and thus purify herself.

f. When a person newly accepts Islam, he should be instructed to carry out total ablution following his proclamation of acceptance.

How to carry out total ablution

Having prepared the water or entered the bath with the object of ritually removing impurities, by tradition you are required to begin by washing your hands three times followed by the cleansing of the private parts. After this one should proceed as in the ritual ablution, except that the legs should be left until the rest of the body has been washed.[24]

Next pour three handfuls of water on your head and pass your fingers through the roots of your hair. You should then pour the water liberally over the body, leaving no part of it untouched.

Having made the resolve to perform the total ablution you may do so by immersion in a river or water and accompany this with the rinsing of the mouth and the inhalation of water into the nostrils.

You may also stand under a shower. Having finished pouring water on your body, finally wash your legs and then begin to dry yourself, praising Allah and giving thanks to Him and seeking His blessing by saying:

«اللهم اجعلني من التوابين واجعلني من المتطهرين»

O Lord, make me repentant, make me clean.

Purification with earth

One of the dispensations of Islam is that Allah does not impose anything upon a soul of which he or she is incapable. Because of the importance of prayer as a pillar of Islam, religion permits neither the abandonment of prayer nor the neglecting or delaying of it. Purification, as you have learned, is a basic requirement and water is the essential cleanser. However, if you have no water, whether on a journey or in an inhabited area, or there is water, but you are ill and fear that its use will definitely cause you severe harm, or if you are not ill but, on awakening in a state of major impurity, you are fearful that total ablution may cause you to suffer the gravest consequences due to severe cold, Allah has in these circumstances substituted good clean earth (or sand) for water. Thus cleansing by the use of earth

smooths your path, allays your fears, and demonstrates concern for prayers, that sturdy pillar of your religion. Read these verse carefully and attentively:

Almightly Allah says:

﴿ يَٰٓأَيُّهَا ٱلَّذِينَ ءَامَنُوٓا۟ إِذَا قُمْتُمْ إِلَى ٱلصَّلَوٰةِ فَٱغْسِلُوا۟ وُجُوهَكُمْ وَأَيْدِيَكُمْ إِلَى ٱلْمَرَافِقِ وَٱمْسَحُوا۟ بِرُءُوسِكُمْ وَأَرْجُلَكُمْ إِلَى ٱلْكَعْبَيْنِ ۚ وَإِن كُنتُمْ جُنُبًا فَٱطَّهَّرُوا۟ ۚ وَإِن كُنتُم مَّرْضَىٰٓ أَوْ عَلَىٰ سَفَرٍ أَوْ جَآءَ أَحَدٌ مِّنكُم مِّنَ ٱلْغَآئِطِ أَوْ لَٰمَسْتُمُ ٱلنِّسَآءَ فَلَمْ تَجِدُوا۟ مَآءً فَتَيَمَّمُوا۟ صَعِيدًا طَيِّبًا فَٱمْسَحُوا۟ بِوُجُوهِكُمْ وَأَيْدِيكُم مِّنْهُ ۚ مَا يُرِيدُ ٱللَّهُ لِيَجْعَلَ عَلَيْكُم مِّنْ حَرَجٍ وَلَٰكِن يُرِيدُ لِيُطَهِّرَكُمْ وَلِيُتِمَّ نِعْمَتَهُۥ عَلَيْكُمْ لَعَلَّكُمْ تَشْكُرُونَ ۝٦ ﴾ [المائدة]

Believers, when you prepare for prayer, wash your faces and your hands to the elbows; rub your heads and your feet to the ankles. If you are in a state of ritual impurity, bathe your whole body. But if you are ill, or on a journey, or one of you comes from the offices of nature, or you have been in contact with women, and you find no water, then take clean sand or earth and rub your faces and hands with it. Allah does not wish to create difficulties for you. He only wants to make you clean, and to complete His favour to you so that you may be grateful.

(*Surah al-Ma'idah*, The Table Spread, 5:6)

The word which the Arabs use for this action means "intention." Hence, when the Muslim cannot find water, he uses earth, sand, or dust with the "intention of cleansing himself. "And it is not required of him that he cover his hands and face with it. If there should be any dust adhering to your hands at the time of purification with earth, first blow it off and then proceed with the purification.

Allah's purpose is to provide a substitute for ritual or total ablution, so that you will not on such occasions out of laziness or forgetfulness, omit to pray—and eventually get out of the habit of praying altogether. In this way Allah demonstrates the importance of prayer to us by stressing that even though there is no water, and even though one may be ill, it is still our duty to say our prayers.

PURIFY OUR HEARTS

Forgive us, Lord, and forgive our brothers who embraced the Faith before us. Do not put in our hearts any malice towards the faithful. Lord, You are Compassionate, and Merciful.

(Surah al-Hashr, Exile, 59:10).

Lord, in You we have put our trust; to You we turn and to You we shall come at last. Lord, do not expose us to the designs of the unbelievers. Forgive us, Lord; You are the Mighty, the Wise One.

(Surah al-Mumtahanah, 60:4-5).

Lord, perfect our light for us and forgive us. You have power over all things.

(Surah al-Tahrim, Prohibited, 66:8).

If a man is revolted at the thought of using earth or dust, and it is contrary to his principles of hygiene—for to put it on the face or on the eyes is something which reason cannot accept—then a Muslim should say to him: "Islam stipulates above all that the dust or earth be clean, wholesome, and unadulterated. This is not harmful even if it gets into the eyes." To some extent the unclean dust, which is swirled and carried by the wind, blows into the eyes every day, but during purification none of it enters the eyes. Purification with earth, sand, or dust, is prescribed only in cases of necessity. It comes as a balm to the soul of the believer who, counting it one of Allah's blessings to the community—a blessing which He has conferred to make it easier for us to follow our religion—endures it as one of the special characteristics of Islamic ritual.

﴿ ..... مَا يُرِيدُ ٱللَّهُ لِيَجْعَلَ عَلَيْكُم مِّنْ حَرَجٍ وَلَٰكِن يُرِيدُ لِيُطَهِّرَكُمْ وَلِيُتِمَّ نِعْمَتَهُۥ عَلَيْكُمْ لَعَلَّكُمْ تَشْكُرُونَ ۝ ﴾ [المائدة]

Allah does not wish to create difficulties for you, but to make you clean, and to complete his favour to you, so that you may be grateful.
(*Surah al-Ma'ida*, The Table Spread, 5:6)

A description of the purification

When forced to purify yourself with earth because there is no available water, look for wholesome dust, either sand or salt sand. First, resolve upon purification by earth, then pronounce the name of Allah saying, "In the name of Allah, the Compassionate, the Merciful."

Then put your open hands, with fingers outstretched, on the dust. Strike the dust with your hands, then raise them. Blowing off the dust which adheres to them, wipe your hands over your face and over the back of the hands up to the wrists. By this action you will be able to perform the prayers, and it will be as if you had carried out the ritual ablution.

If you should awake in a state of major impurity and there is no water to be found, purifying yourself by earth in this way will absolve you from defilement and excuse you from total ablution. However, you must resolve in your heart to be rid of the defilement and pronounce the name of Allah when purifying yourself.

Purification by earth has the same validity as ritual ablution, but becomes invalid when water is found. Until your ritual purification is broken or until water is found, it is lawful for you, with one purification by earth, to perform any of the obligatory or voluntary prayers. Some theologians hold the opinion that purification by earth should be done by striking the dust twice, once for the face and once for the hands.

Removing dirt

Anyone saying his prayers must perform it wearing clean clothes. In addition, the place in which the prayers are to be performed should be clean as well. Should there be dirt on any of these things, he must remove it with water, cleaning the affected part and removing the stain. Foulness which must be removed includes urine, excrement, fresh semen (dry semen may be brushed off), the saliva of a dog, etc., blood and suppurative matter.

A woman must remove all traces of her menstrual period when it ends and perform total ablution. She must do the same after childbirth. Prayers are not performed during her menstrual period. She must do the same after childbirth. She must not say her prayers during the time of post-natal haemorrhage, even though this for lasts forty days. However, she must observe the fast. The Qur'an has this to say:

﴿ وَيَسْـَٔلُونَكَ عَنِ ٱلْمَحِيضِ قُلْ هُوَ أَذًى فَٱعْتَزِلُوا۟ ٱلنِّسَآءَ فِى ٱلْمَحِيضِ وَلَا تَقْرَبُوهُنَّ حَتَّىٰ يَطْهُرْنَ فَإِذَا تَطَهَّرْنَ فَأْتُوهُنَّ مِنْ حَيْثُ أَمَرَكُمُ ٱللَّهُ إِنَّ ٱللَّهَ يُحِبُّ ٱلتَّوَّٰبِينَ وَيُحِبُّ ٱلْمُتَطَهِّرِينَ ۝ ﴾ [البقرة]

They ask you about menstruation. Say: It is an indisposition so keep away from women during their menstrual periods, and do not approach them until they are clean. But when they have purified themselves, you may approach them, in any manner, time or place ordained for you by Allah. For Allah loves those who keep themselves pure and clean.

(*Surah al-Baqarah*, The Heifer, 2:222)

B. The time of prayer

1. General

A Muslim may not perform the obligatory prayers until the arrival of the proper hour as stated in the Law. The Qur'an says:

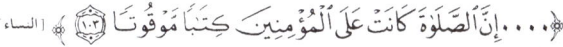

Prayers are enjoined at the stated times.

(*Surah al-Nisa*, The Woman, 4:103)

This means that there is a pre-established obligatory religious duty for which the Qur'an has set fixed times. The arrival of the time for prayer is a fundamental condition for performing it. The times are :

a. The morning prayer

This prayer begins at true dawn, which occurs in the east when the light first appears from the darkness of night and extends until the sun rises. He who has completed one rak'ah of the morning prayer before sunrise has performed the prayer on time. He who oversleeps and awakens after the appointed time should perform it immediately upon waking and not delay his duty. Furthermore, he must not oversleep intentionally or be lazy in getting out of his bed, for whoever does this suffers manifest loss.

b. The noon prayer

This prayer will normally be at twelve o'clock noon, but the time varies in different countries. The time for the noon prayer lasts until the time for the afternoon prayer.

c. The afternoon prayer

This is enjoined when the shadow of an object is equal to its own length plus the length of its noontime shadow. The time for this prayer extends until sunset. He who has completed one rak'ah of the afternoon prayer has performed the rite in time, but one is not permitted to delay the prayer until the sun turns yellow (or red or orange). Should the time for this prayer be over, his efforts will be rendered valueless, as is stated in a Tradition.[25]

The afternoon prayer is the middle one, which is mentioned in the following verse :

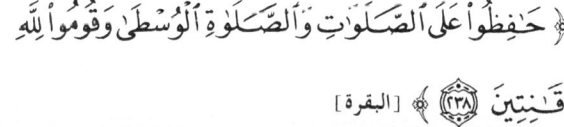

Keep strictly to your (habit) of prayer,
Especially the middle prayer,[26] and stand
before Allah in a devout (frame of mind).

(*Surah al-Baqarah,* The Heifer, 2:238)

d. The sunset prayers

This prayer may be performed from sunset until the end of twilight. Twilight is the redness which remains on the horizon after the sun sets and lasts until the onset of darkness. The interval allowed for the sunset prayer is the shortest of all and it is advisable to lose no time in performing it.

e. The evening prayers

This begins when twilight ends, although the interval for it extends until daybreak.

The Prophet disliked sleeping before this prayer or conversing after it. Conversation after dark was permitted only for the sake of acquiring knowledge or to honour a guest, and it was preferable to delay the evening prayer until a third of the night had passed. However, if it is feared that the time for prayer will be missed should it be delayed, it must be performed at once.

The times for the five prayers have been laid down by Islam. They never change, nor do they vary with the seasons of the year. It is possible to regulate the afternoon hours by the calls of the *muezzins* in the mosques, which keep you informed of the times for prayer in both summer and winter.[27]

If the time for the evening prayer has arrived, but the evening meal is ready, eat it and perform the prayer afterwards with a peaceful and tranquil mind. Note also that the Prophet has forbidden you to go the prayer while needing to relieve yourself.

2. The call to prayer

The call to prayer is the signal that the time for obeisance has arrived. Through the use of the prescribed words the Muslim community is summoned to attend to those prayers which will lead to their prosperity in this life and the hereafter.

The call to prayer is in itself an act of worship which precedes the prayers and, as such, is one of the most important religious ceremonics in Islam, and the most widely recognized characteristic of the religion. It was introduced in the first year of the Hijra[28], following which the Prophet observed it night and day, whether at home or travelling. On no occasion until the day of his death was it known of him to break the custom, nor is there any known instance in which he granted a dispensation from the rule. The Companions continued to observe the rule until it became a duty, or the equivalent of a duty because of the Prophet's order which is preserved in a number of Traditions.

THE MOSQUE

Whereas there is a plethora of old forts in most countries, they are remarkably scarce in Muslim lands. The skyline of Muslim towns is dominated more by the lofty minarets of mosques. This shows the difference between the Islamic and non-Islamic temperament. Non-Muslims rely on their own strategies; Muslims place total trust in Allah. This explains why non-Muslims have always erected forts for their own protection and security, while Muslims have built mosques wherever they achieved supremacy. Massive castles testify to man's greatness, whereas mosques, in which Muslims glorify Allah, are a reminder to present and future generations of the greatness of Allah.

A mosque is, locally, a focal point for Muslims, just as the Ka'bah in Makkah is for Muslims all over the world. The Ka'bah is a world religious centre and the mosque a local one. That is why the same word for the direction in which one faces to pray—*qiblah* has been used in the Qur'an for both the Holy Ka'bah and also local mosques. Prayer is a symbol of a life of faith, and houses of worship, mosques, are for the performance of that act of faith on a local level and, in the case of Makkah and Madinah, on an international level.

Muslims gather five times a day to pray in the mosque. The mosque is their natural religious centre. That is why the Prophet encouraged us to build mosques in the centres of towns. The situation of mosques, and the activities which are conducted in them, are in themselves an invitation to people to come together for worship of their Lord.

— *Introducing Islam* by Maulana Wahiduddin Khan

3. A description of the call to prayer

The call to Prayer, as is stated in authentic Traditions, is as follows:

اللهُ أَكْبَرُ ، اللهُ أَكْبَرُ ، اللهُ أَكْبَرُ ، اللهُ أَكْبَرُ

Allah is Great, Allah is Great, Allah is Great, Allah is Great.

أَشْهَدُ أَنْ لا إله إلاَّ اللّه

I bear witness that there is no deity save Allah.

أَشْهَدُ أَنْ لا إله إلاَّ اللّه

I bear witness that there is no deity save Allah.

أَشْهَدُ أَنْ مُحَمَّداً رسُولُ الله

I bear witness that Muhammad is the Messenger of Allah.

أَشْهَدُ أَنْ مُحَمَّداً رسُولُ الله

I bear witness that Muhammad is the Messenger of Allah.

حَيَّ على الصَّلاة ، حَيَّ على الصَّلاة

Come to prayer. Come to prayer.

حَيَّ على الفَلاحِ ، حَيَّ على الفَلاحِ

Come to prosperity. Come to prosperity.

اللهُ أَكْبَرُ ، اللهُ أَكْبَرُ

Allah is Great. Allah is Great.

لا إلهَ إلا اللهُ

There is no deity save Allah.

In the morning prayer only, after saying "come to prosperity" (حيَّ على الفــــلاح) and before saying, for the second time, "Allah is Great, Allah is Great", the *muezzin* adds:

«الصَّلاةُ خَيْرٌ مِنَ النَّومِ ، الصَّلاةُ خَيْرٌ مِنَ النَّومِ»

Prayer is better than sleep.
Prayer is better than sleep.

Then he continues with:

Allah is Great. Allah is Great,
There is no deity save Allah.

Notes: When you hear the sound of the call to Prayer reverberating in the air, let your heart be filled with the magnificence of the call and the glory of Him in whose name the call is made. Realize that, apart from Him, there is nothing great. Remember—only Allah is Great, only Allah is Great.

When you hear the *meuzzin*, pay attention to him. Repeat what he says in your heart with all the power you possess, until he says:

Come to prayer. Come to prosperity.

حيَّ على الصَّلاة ، حيَّ على الفلاح

At this point say, "There is no power and no strength except in Allah. There is no power and no strength except in Allah".

لا حَوْلَ وَلا قُوَّةَ إلا بالله

Listen to the Tradition of the glorious Messenger of Allah as related in *al-Bhukhari*.[29] The Prophet says: "When the *muezzin* says 'Allah is Great' say 'Allah is Great' then he says, "I bear witness that there is no deity but Allah,' say, 'I bear witness that there is no deity but Allah." When he says, 'I bear witness that Muhammad is the Messenger of Allah', say, 'I bear witness that Muhammad is the Messenger of Allah. There is no power and no strength except in Allah.' When he says, 'Allah is Great, Allah is Great', say, 'Allah is Great, Allah is Great.' When he says, 'There is no deity save Allah, say, 'There is no deity save Allah.' If this is said from the heart you will enter paradise."

When you have finished answering the *muezzin*, ask the blessing of the Prophet. Then request Allah's favour for him in the words of the traditional private prayer. Turn your mind to the humility of the glorious Messenger, all of whose sins Allah has forgiven. He calls on his people to bless him and entreat Him to grant His favour to him after each call to prayer, so that mankind will turn to Allah and Allah alone, and learn that all things are for Allah to do as He wishes and as He chooses, for man, no matter how exalted his rank or authority, is but the slave of the Compassionate, the

Merciful of whom he is always in need. Abdullah ibn Amr, as related by Imam Muslim,[30] said that he had heard the Messenger of Allah say:

> *When you hear the meuzzin, say what he says, then ask a blessing for me. Whoever asks a blessing for me once, will be blessed ten times by Allah. Then ask Allah for His favour to me, which is a position in paradise, which can only be aspired to by a slave of Allah. Would that I am the one. He who asks Allah's favour for me, for him will I intercede.*

The traditional private prayer which is said after each call to prayer is that which our Prophet has taught us and is as follows:

«اللَّهُمَّ رَبَّ هَذِهِ الدَّعْوَةِ التَّامَّةِ، وَالصَّلَاةِ القَائِمَةِ آتِ مُحَمَّداً الوَسِيلَةَ وَالفَضِيلَةَ وَابْعَثْهُ مَقَاماً مَحْمُوداً الَّذِي وَعَدْتَهُ»

O Allah, Lord of all supplications and steadfast prayer, grant Muhammad the most favoured and excellent position. Admit him to the Praiseworthy Place that You have promised him.[31]

Then say,

«وَارْزُقْنَا شَفَاعَتَهُ إِنَّكَ لَا تُخْلِفُ الْمِيعَادَ»

Bestow upon us his intercession, for You do not fail in Your promise.[32]

4. The second call (iqama)

After the *muezzin* has made the call to prayer, it is the traditional law that there shall be an interval until the second call, during which the worshipper should make ready for the prayer. He who makes the call begins when all the necessary conditions for performing the prayer are fulfilled. When this is done and all is ready for prayer, stand facing the direction of the Ka'bah, make the second call, and then perform the prayer.

5. How to make the second call

There are two correct methods of giving the second call.

a. The first method:

This consists of eleven sentences:

اللهُ أكْبَرُ ، اللهُ أكْبَرُ

Allah is Great, Allah is Great.

أَشْهَدُ أَنْ لا إِلهَ إِلاَّ الله

I bear witness that there is no deity save Allah.

أَشْهَدُ أَنْ مُحَمَّداً رَسُولُ الله

I bear witness that Muhammad is the Messenger of Allah.

حَيَّ على الصَّلاة

Come to prayer.

حَيَّ على الفلاحِ

Come to prosperity.

قد قامت الصلاة ، قد قامت الصلاة

The prayer is to be performed.
The prayer is to be performed.

اللهُ أكْبَرُ ، اللهُ أكْبَرُ

Allah is Great. Allah is Great.

لا إله إلاَّ الله

There is no deity save Allah.

b. The second method:

This consists of seventeen sentences with the first "Allah is Great" being repeated four times and all other sentences but the last being said twice. Finally, the statement "There is no deity save Allah" is made once. Here is the entire call:

اللهُ أكبرُ ، اللهُ أكبرُ ، اللهُ أكبرُ ، اللهُ أكبرُ

Allah is Great, Allah is Great, Allah is Great, Allah is Great.

أشْهَدُ أنْ لا إله إلاَّ الله

I bear witness that there is no deity save Allah.

أشْهدُ أنْ لا إله إلاَّ الله

I bear witness that there is no deity save Allah.

أشْهَدُ أنْ مُحمَّداً رسُولُ الله

I bear witness that Muhammad is the Messenger of Allah.

أشْهدُ أنْ مُحمَّداً رسُولُ الله

I bear witness that Muhammad is the Messenger of Allah.

حيَّ على الصَّلاة ، حيَّ على الصَّلاة

Come to prayer, come to prayer.

حيَّ على الفلاح ، حيَّ على الفلاح

Come to prosperity, come to prosperity.

قد قامت الصلاة ، قد قامت الصلاة

The prayer is to be performed, the prayer is to be performed.

اللهُ أكبرُ ، اللهُ أكبرُ

Allah is great, Allah is great.

لا إله إلاَّ الله

There is no deity save Allah.

Notes :

1. It is traditional for the *muezzin* to make the call to prayer in a slow and unhurried fashion, with a pause between each two invocations; the second call should be made rapidly and that there should be no talking in the course of the invocation.

2. During the call to prayer one should face towards the Ka'bah, saying it aloud, even though one is alone in the desert.

3. If you miss the prayer due to oversleeping or forgetfulness, then you should recite to yourself both the call to prayer and the second call when you perform the prayer. If you have missed a number of prayers, it is preferable that you recite at least the call to prayer and the second call for the first prayer, but only the second call for each of the other prayers.

4. The call to prayer and the second call are not obligatory for women, but if they should give them, there is no harm in it, as has been stated by Imam Ahmed ibn Hanbal.

Aisha, as related by *al-Bayhaqi*,[33] used to give the first and second calls to prayers, leading the women in prayer and standing in the midst.

5. The listener should repeat the words of the *muezzin* in the second call as he does in the first call to prayer, except where the muezzin says:

حيَّ على الصَّلاة ، حيَّ على الفلاح

Come to prayer, come to prosperity.

Here the listener says :

لا حوْل ولا قُوَّةَ إلا بالله

There is no power or strength except in Allah.

When the *muezzin* says:

قد قامت الصلاة

The prayer is to be performed.

The listener says:

أقامها الله وأدامَها

May Allah raise it up and make it last forever.[34]

Facing the direction of the Ka'bah

Islam is the religion of unity and monotheism. There is one Allah, one Book, and one direction to face. Muslims of the East and of the West look not only with their eyes but with their hearts towards the Ka'bah, the symbol of unity and the source of the radiant light of Muhammad (peace be upon him). All who perform the prayer must face towards the Ka'bah in the holy city of Makkah in accordance with the word of Allah:

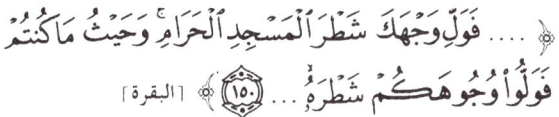

[البقرة]

Whichever way you depart, face in the direction of the Sacred Mosque, and wherever you are, face towards it.

(Surah al-Baqarah, The Heifer, 2:150)

He who can actually see the Ka'bah should look directly at it. All that one can do, if it is not visible, is to face in its direction, for Allah does not place an undue burden upon anyone. Our forefathers in every country have determined the direction of the Ka'bah and have pointed the *Qibla* of the mosques towards it. You can therefore determine the direction of the Ka'bah in your house by reference to the mosque. Alternatively, you may use a compass or judge by the stars at night. When you face the Pole star, for instance, you always face north and the direction of the Ka'bah may be worked out from this.

2. The rule when the direction of the Ka'bah cannot be determined

Anyone who is unable to find the direction of the Ka'bah because, for instance, of clouds or darkness, must ask someone who does know to indicate the right direction. But if there is no one to ask, then he must decide for himself which is the right direction and perform the prayers facing that way. His prayer will still be correct and will not require repetition should it be discovered, after the prayer is completed, that he was in error. Should the mistake be pointed out while the prayers are in progress, he should turn towards the proper direction without interrupting his prayer.

Should you be performing the prayer in the direction which you think most likely to be correct, but it is suggested by some more knowledgeable person that you should face such and such a direction, then do turn to it. This movement and change of direction will not render the prayer invalid. This has been established by Ibn 'Umar, as related by *al-Bukhari* and *Muslim*,[35] who said:

"While the people of Quba' were performing the morning prayer, a man came upon them and said: 'Last night, the Qur'an was revealed to the Prophet (may Allah bless him and grant him peace) and he was commanded to turn towards the Ka'bah. So turn towards it.' They were facing Syria,[36] so they turned towards the Ka'bah."

If the direction of the Ka'bah remains unknown for a long time, the worshipper should ascertain the direction each time he performs the prayer. Should he change his mind, he should then follow his new decision, but the prayers already performed need not be repeated.

3. When is the direction of the Ka'bah not faced?

Facing the direction of the Ka'bah is a religious duty which may not be dispensed with except in certain circumstances:

1. When in fear, peril, or sickness, it is permitted to perform the prayer in a direction other than that of the Ka'bah, should it be impossible to face it absolutely. The religion of Islam is not burdensome. The Prophet says, "If I command you to do something, do what you are able to."[37]

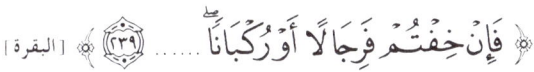

When you are exposed to danger, pray on foot, or while riding.

(Surah al-Baqarah, The Heifer, 2:239)

Al-Bukhari relates that Ibn Umar said, " Pray facing the direction of the Ka'bah, or otherwise."[38]

2. It is permissible for a rider to perform a supererogatory prayer on his mount by going through the motions of bowing and prostrating. The movements which indicate the prostrations should be lower than those of the bows. The direction he faces is that of the animal he is riding. The same thing holds for a passenger on a ship, an airplane or a train. He begins to pray by facing the direction of the Ka'bah, and continues the prayers in the same position, even though the direction in which he is travelling changes.

Imam Ahmad, Al-Tirmidhi, and Muslim all relate[39] that the Prophet used to perform the prayers while mounted, when travelling from Makkah to Madina, regardless of the direction he faced. As the Quran declares'.

﴿ فَأَيْنَمَا تُوَلُّوا فَثَمَّ وَجْهُ اللَّهِ ..... ﴾ (١١٥) [البقرة]

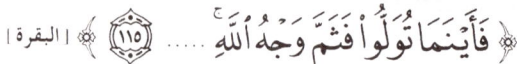

Whichever way you turn, there is the presence of Allah.

(*Surah al-Baqarah*, The Heifer, 2:115)

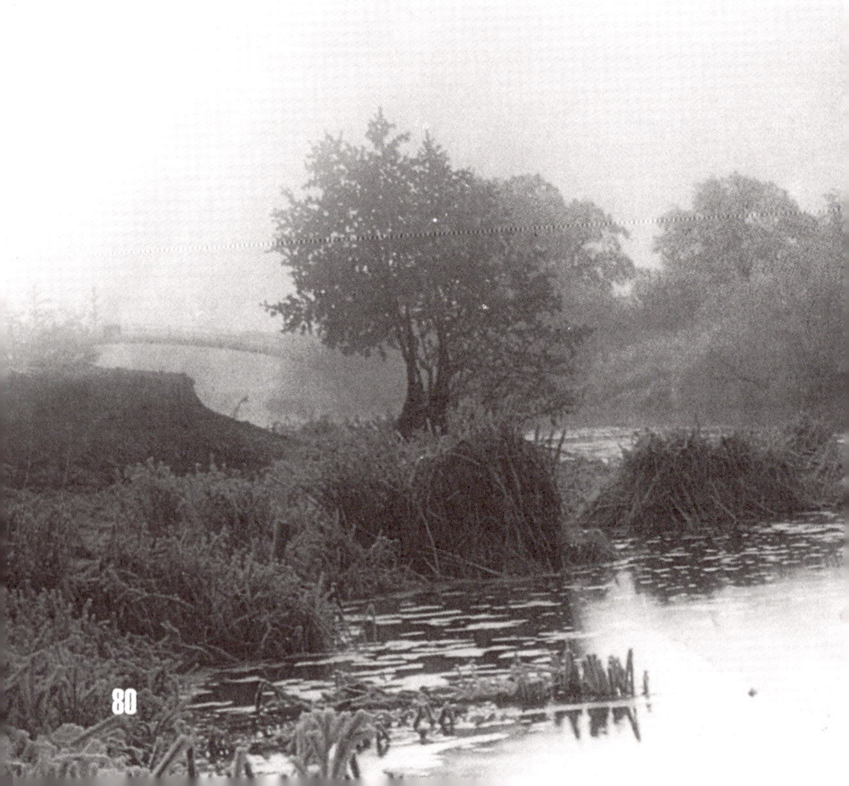

This was the Prophet's custom with supererogatory prayers, but not with those which were obligatory.[40]

Three

How the prayers are performed

We have seen what is to be done before commencing the prayers. These practices, adhered to since the time of the Prophet, have been handed down to his successors. Where we wish to begin the prayers, how do we perform it, and what are the relevant duties?

The time for the prayer having arrived, first fulfil all the conditions for cleanliness and dressing. Now, stand with your eyes facing towards the Ka'bah and your heart facing towards Allah. Dedicate your intentions and actions to Him and resolve upon the prayer to Him.

Prepare your heart and let your soul be in fear of the Lord, for you are about to stand before the Master of Heaven and Earth. Call to mind the majesty and glory of Allah. The more intense your remembrance of Him, the greater will be your dread. Then do the following:

1. Commence the prayer with the Words of Greatness, that is (الله أكبر) "Allah is Great", while at the time raising the open hands and placing the thumbs behind the lobes of the ears.

2. Then place the right hand over the left and put them together on your chest.

3. After this, recite the private prayer which is called the Opening and Facing Allah Prayer.

This may be any of those with which the Prophet used to commence the prayer after saying the Words of Greatness and before reciting the *Surah al-Fatihah*.[41]

Here are three of the private prayers which the Prophet used. You should memorize one of them and use it as the Opening Prayer each time the prayers are performed.

a. The first private prayer:

١ـ « سُبْحَانَكَ اللَّهُمَّ ، وَبِحَمْدِكَ ، وَتَبَارَكَ اسْمُكَ ، وَتَعَالَى جَدُّكَ ، وَلَا إِلَهَ غَيْرُكَ » .

Praise and glory be to Allah. Blessed be Your name. Exalted be Your Majesty and Glory. There is no deity save You.[42]

b. The second private prayer:

٢ـ «اَللّهُمَّ باعِدْ بَيْني وَبَيْنَ خَطايايَ كَما باعَدْتَ بَيْنَ المَشْرِقِ وَالمَغْرِبِ، اَللّهُمَّ نَقِّني مِنْ خَطايايَ كَما يُنَقّى الثَوْبُ الأَبْيَضُ مِنَ الدَنَسِ، اَللّهُمَّ اغْسِلْني مِنْ خَطايايَ بِالماءِ وَالثَلْجِ وَالبَرَدِ».

O Lord, separate me from my sins as You have separated the east and the west. O Lord, cleanse me of my sins as the white robe is cleansed from dirt. O Lord, wash away my sins with water, snow, and hail.[43]

c. The third private prayer

٣ـ «إِنّي وَجَّهْتُ وَجْهِيَ لِلَّذي فَطَرَ السَّمواتِ وَالأَرْضَ حَنيفاً مُسْلِماً وَما أَنا مِنَ المُشْرِكينَ، إِنَّ صَلاتي وَنُسُكي وَمَحْيايَ وَمَماتي لِلّهِ رَبِّ العالَمينَ لا شَريكَ لَهُ، وَبِذلِكَ أُمِرْتُ وَأَنا مِنَ المُسْلِمينَ»

I turn my face to Him Who has created heaven and earth, as a true believer and a Muslim, and not one of the polytheists. My prayer and my devoutness belong to Allah, Lord of the worlds, Who has no partner. Therefore am I commanded and therefore do I submit.[44]

We will content ourselves with this portion of the prayer. The Prophet used to recite it at the voluntary evening prayer only,⁴⁵ but the Tradition in full (as related by Imam Ahmad and Muslim) concludes:

«اللَّهُمَّ أَنْتَ المَلِكُ لا إِلهَ إِلا أَنْتَ، أَنْتَ رَبِّي وَأَنَا عَبْدُكَ، ظَلَمْتُ نَفْسِي، وَاعْتَرَفْتُ بِذَنْبِي فَاغْفِرْ لِي ذُنُوبِي جَمِيعًا، إِنَّهُ لا يَغْفِرُ الذُّنُوبَ إِلا أَنْتَ، وَاهْدِنِي لِأَحْسَنِ الأَخْلاقِ، لا يَهْدِي لِأَحْسَنِهَا إِلا ات، وَاصْرِفْ عَنِّي سَيِّئَهَا، لا يَصْرِفُ عَنِّي سَيِّئَهَا إِلا أَنْتَ، لَبَّيْكَ وَسَعْدَيْكَ، وَالخَيْرُ كُلُّهُ فِي يَدَيْكَ وَالشَّرُّ لَيْسَ إِلَيْكَ، وَأَنَا بِكَ وَإِلَيْكَ، تَبَارَكْتَ وَتَعَالَيْتَ أَسْتَغْفِرُكَ وَأَتُوبُ إِلَيْكَ».

*O Lord You are the Kind One, There is no deity save You. You are my Master and I am Your servant. I have done wrong. I acknowledge my sins. Only You can forgive sins. Guide me to the finest moral character. Only You can guide me to the best. Turn away an evil nature. Only You can turn away its evil. I obey You and rejoice in You. All prosperity is in Your hands and there can be no evil in You. I am Yours and belong to You. You are blessed and exalted. I seek Your forgiveness and turn to You in repentance.*⁴⁶

ALL PRAISE IS DUE TO ALLAH

A tree is unaware of its own extraordinary significance. A flower does not realize what a delicate and exquisite masterpiece it really is. A bird is oblivious to its own breathtaking beauty. Though all things in this world are classic specimens of the most exquisite art, they never come to know themselves as such.

For whom, then, is this beautiful and gracious display? It is all for man's benefit. Man is the only being in the known universe who can perceive beauty in a thing and appreciate its excellence. Allah has created exquisite works of art in worldly form and enabled man to apprehend them. He has given man a tongue to express his wonder at and veneration of Allah's stupendous feats of creation. What he utters is praise, or admiration of Allah. It is a tribute of the most sublime sentiments, expressed in human words and offered to Allah.

Praise means being moved at the sight of Allah's craftsmanship and spontaneously expressing one's realization of His perfection. "Allah, all praise is due to You. You are chaste and exalted. Allah, count me among the believers, and raise me not up blind like those who failed to acknowledge your perfection or perceive Your beauty." Praise is constant remembrance of Allah in this manner, in Arabic or in any other language.

— *Introducing Islam* by Maulana Wahiduddin Khan

4. Having said the Opening Prayer, seek the protection of Allah before beginning the recitation of the Qur'an. "I seek the protection of Allah from the accursed Satan."

أعوذ بالله من الشيطان الرجيم

This is to be said only at the start of the first rak'a.

In subsequent rak'ahs it is sufficient to say, "In the name of Allah, the Compassionate, the Merciful."

بسم الله الرحمن الرحيم

This should also be said after seeking Allah's protection from Satan.

5. Then recite the Opening Verses of the Qur'an, reflecting and pondering on their meaning.

بِسْمِ ٱللَّهِ ٱلرَّحْمَٰنِ ٱلرَّحِيمِ ﴿١﴾ ٱلْحَمْدُ لِلَّهِ رَبِّ ٱلْعَٰلَمِينَ ﴿٢﴾
ٱلرَّحْمَٰنِ ٱلرَّحِيمِ ﴿٣﴾ مَٰلِكِ يَوْمِ ٱلدِّينِ ﴿٤﴾ إِيَّاكَ نَعْبُدُ وَإِيَّاكَ
نَسْتَعِينُ ﴿٥﴾ ٱهْدِنَا ٱلصِّرَٰطَ ٱلْمُسْتَقِيمَ ﴿٦﴾ صِرَٰطَ ٱلَّذِينَ أَنْعَمْتَ
عَلَيْهِمْ غَيْرِ ٱلْمَغْضُوبِ عَلَيْهِمْ وَلَا ٱلضَّآلِّينَ ﴿٧﴾ [الفاتحة]

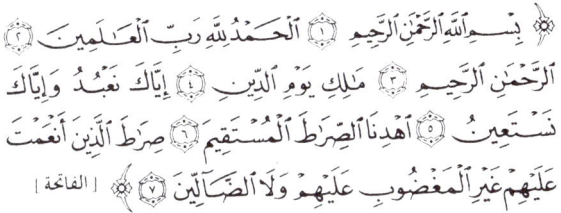

Praise be to Allah, Lord of the Universe, the Compassionate, the Merciful, Master of the Day of Judgement! You alone we worshing and to You alone we turn for help. Show us the straight path. The way of those on whom You have bestowed Your Grace, not of those who have incurred Your wrath, nor of those who have gone astray.

(*Surah al-Fatihah,* The Opening, 1:1-7)

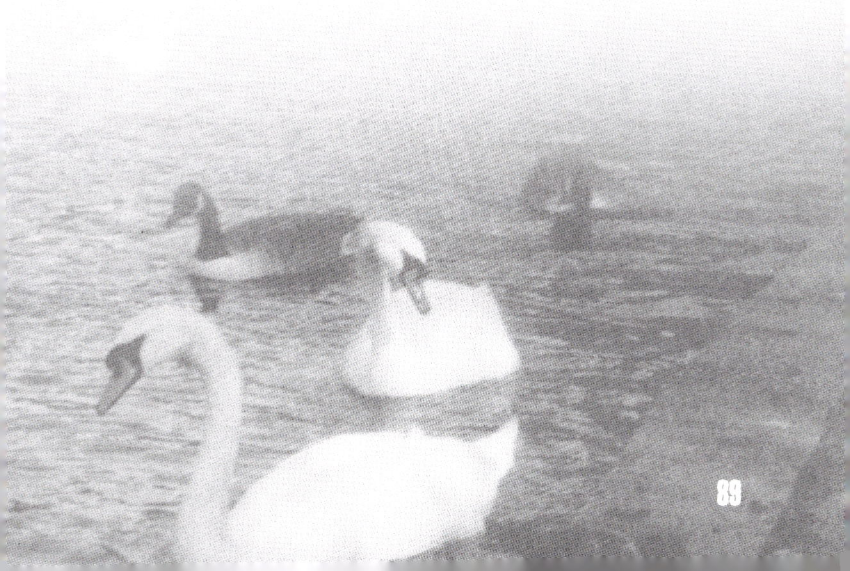

It is the traditional law that each person who performs the prayers, be he an Imam, or a worshipper on his own, or accompanied by an Imam, must say "Amen" آمين immediately after reciting this chapter. Say it aloud where the prayer is said aloud and whisper it when the prayer is said quietly. The mosques used to shake and resound to the cry of "Amen" coming from the throats and hearts of the devout slaves of Allah.

"Amen" is itself a prayer which means

"O Lord, answer my prayer."

6. After reciting the Opening Verses of the Qur'an,[47] tradition requires you to recite one of the short chapters of the Quran or at least three verses from any portion of the Qur'an. Tradition also requires that this recitation takes place after reciting the Opening verses in the two *rak'ahs* of the noon, afternoon, sunset, and evening prayers, and in every rak'ah of the supererogatory or voluntary prayers.

7. At the end of the recitation of the Opening Verses of the Qur'an and whatever you might recite after it, say the Words of Greatness, الله أكبر then bow. It is preferable to raise your hands[48] alongside your ears and, during the bow, to lower them down to the knees. Tradition holds that the head should be level with the buttocks, and that you should support yourself by putting your hands on your knees, keeping them away from your sides.

The fingers on the knees and legs should be wide apart and

your back should be straight. While bowing, praise the name of Allah, saying, "Praise be to my Glorious Lord."

(سُبْحَان رَبِّي العظيم).

This should be done three times.

8. Stand upright from the bowing position. It is recommended that you raise your hands alongside your ears. While straightening up, whether you are the Imam, with the Imam, or alone say, "May Allah hear the one who praises Him."

سمع الله لمن حمده

When finally upright, say: "Our Lord be praised."

ربَنا ولك الْحمدُ

This is the minimum to which you may confine yourself in words of praise when straightening up from bowing and it is preferable to add to these words whatever has been established by genuine Tradition. For example:

(سمع الله لمن حمده ربنا ولك الحمد، حمدًا كثيرًا، طيبا، مباركًا فيه)

May Allah hear the one who praises Him.
Our Lord be praised, with much praise,
goodness and blessing.[49]

(سَمِعَ اللهُ لِمَنْ حَمِدَه ، رَبَّنَا وَلَكَ الْحَمْدُ مِلْءَ السَّمٰوَاتِ وَالْأَرْضِ وَمَا بَيْنَهُمَا ، وَمِلْءَ مَا شِئْتَ مِنْ شَيْءٍ بَعْدُ)

May Allah hear the one who praises Him. O Lord, the praise which fills heaven and earth, all that is between them and whatever You wish to be filled, is Yours.[50]

9. Having straightened from the bow, sink to the ground in prostration, first on to the knees, with the hands well in front of them. Then place the palms of your hands on the ground with the fingers close together in a natural position and put your forehead between your hands. Your feet should be upright during the prostration and must not be raised from the ground. The tips of the toes must point towards the Ka'bah and the bottom of the toes must be in contact with the ground. Do not let the upper part of the foot touch the ground. You must prostrate yourself with absolute humility, remembering always that you have come close to your Lord. While you are prostrated say, "Praise be to You, Exalted Lord!" (سُبْحَانَ رَبِّيَ الْأَعْلٰى) three times.

You may not recite this fewer than three times. However, you may say it more often if you are alone, in which case it is recommended that you say it ten times.[51]

It is also recommended that you should not confine yourself to this phrase, but should add a personal prayer. This is because the Prophet said:

"The servant is nearest to his Lord when prostrating himself. Therefore, increase the personal prayer."[52]

The following are some of the personal prayers the Prophet used to say while prostrating himself.

١ـ اللهم لك سجدت وبك آمنت ولك أسلمت ، سجد وجهي للذي خلقه فصوره ، فأحسن صوره فشق سمعه وبصره فتبارك الله أحسن الخالقين .

O Lord, I prostrate myself before You. In You I believe and to You I submit. I bow down my head to Him who has created and fashioned it, Who has made its form good, Who has brought hearing and sight to it. Allah be praised, how excellent a Creator![53]

٢ـ رب أعط نفسي تقواها ، وزكِّها أنت خير من زكاها أنت وليها ومولاها

O Lord, give my soul devoutness. Purify it. No one but You can purify it. You are its Lord and Master.[54]

٣ـ اللهم إني أعوذ برضاك من سخطك وأعوذ بمعافاتك من عقوبتك وأعوذ بك منك لا أحصي ثناء عليك أنت كما أثنيت على نفسك .

O Lord, I seek the protection of Your favour from Your wrath. I seek refuge in Your protection from Your punishment. I seek refuge in You from Yourself. I cannot count the praises of You, as You have described Yourself.[55]

٤ - اللهم اغفر لي خطيئتي وجهلي وإسرافي في أمري وما أنت أعلم به مني ، اللهم اغفر لي جدّي وخطئي ، وعمدي وكل ذلك عندي ، اللهم اغفر لي ما قدمت وما أخرت ، وما أسررت وما أعلنت ، أنت إلهي ، لا إله إلا أنت .

O Lord, forgive me my sins, my ignorance, my excesses and that of which You know more than I do. O Lord, forgive me my wealth, my error, my intention, and all that is in me. O Lord, forgive me for what I have done and for what I have not done; for what I have kept secret and what I have done openly. You are my Allah. There is no deity save You.[56]

These then are some of the personal prayers which the Prophet used to say during his prostrations. It is recommended that you should learn some of these by heart and say them, following the example of the great Messenger of Allah. Also, during your prostration, you should pray privately about religious and other matters which concern you.

10. After the tranquillity of the prostration, the, person performing the prayers raises his head, saying, "Allah is great." (الله أكبر)

GLORIFYING THE LORD

You who are wrapped up in your vestment, arise and give warning, glorify your Lord, purify your inner self. Keep away from all pollution. Be patient, for your Lord's sake. The day when the trumpet sounds should not be an easy one for the unbelievers; it shall be a day of anguish for them.

(*Surah al-Muddathir,* The Cloaked One, 74:1-10).

No, by the moon! By the departing night and the rising dawn, Hell is a dire scourge, a warning to mankind; alike to those of you who would advance and those who would hang back. Each soul is the hostage of its own deeds. But those on the right hand—they will be in their gardens, inquiring of the sinners; "What brought you into the Fire?" They will reply: "We never prayed or fed the hungry. We engaged in vain disputes and denied the Day of Reckoning until death overtook us." No intercessor's plea shall avail them then.

(*Surah al-Muddathir,* The Cloaked One, 74:32-48).

Then, laying the left foot flat on the ground, he sits back on it, keeping his right foot in its original position with the tips of the toes pointing towards the Ka'bah. He puts his right hand on his right thigh and his left hand on his left thigh, with his fingers in a natural position close to the knees. He sits composedly, then prostrates himself, again saying, "Allah is Great." (الله أكبر)

The second prostration, the words which are said, and the personal prayer, are exactly the same as in the first prostration. It is recommended that you say the following personal prayer between the two prostrations:

« اللهم اغفر لي ، وارحمني ، واعف عني ، وعافني ، وارزقني ، واجبرني ، واسترني »

O Lord, forgive me, have mercy upon me, pardon me, heal me, provide for me, console me, and be a shield for me.[57]

11. When you have completed the second prostration, raise your head, saying, "Allah is Great." This prostration completes one *rak'ah*.[58]

Note: Learn the elements of the *rak'ah* by heart until you have mastered them in every detail, for they are the very essence of the prayers. A thorough grasp of these details is essential to your understanding of further explanations of the prayers.

THE FIVE PRAYERS

For Muslims Allah has prescribed the performance of prayers five times a day. In this way they are cleansed and their hearts are purified. They are linked with Almighty Allah, keeping Him in their minds constantly and everlastingly. Only the devout and pious enjoy the rapture of this meeting and taste the sweetness of faith and worship. Allah has promised that whoever performs these prayers will enter paradise. He who does not perform the prayers has no such promise and Allah will punish him or forgive him as He wishes. The five prayers are as good as fifty and good deeds are rewarded tenfold.

The five prayers contain both the obligatory religious duties and the voluntary prayers imposed by the Traditions of the Prophet. The obligatory duties comprise seventeen rak'ahs a day; two at the morning prayer, three at the sunset prayer, and four each at the noon, afternoon, and night prayers. For the performance of these prayers one is justly rewarded; for their neglect one is rightfully punished. These are the prayers which are prescribed by the Qur'an.

THE VOLUNTARY PRAYERS

The voluntary prayers number twelve rak'ahs, six at the noon prayer and two at the end of the morning, sunset and evening prayers. Through these prayers the believer will be rewarded and through them he draws closer to Allah. However, one will not be punished for their neglect. The Prophet always paid strict attention to the voluntary prayers, In him we have a fine example and must ourselves pay attention to and be guided by him—for this Allah has commanded us to do:

> *So take what the Messenger assigns to you, and deny yourselves whatever he withholds from you.*
>
> (*Surah al-Hashr*, Exile, 59:7)

We shall now explain in detail the five prayers together with the number of obligatory and voluntary *rak'ahs*.

THE MORNING PRAYER (FAJR)

On waking up in the morning make the profession of Faith: "I bear witness that there is no deity save Allah. I bear witness that Muhammad is the Messenger of Allah." Then praise Allah who gives you life after death, saying:

«الحمدُ لله الذى أماتني ثم أحياني وإليه النشور»

Praise be to Allah who has caused me to die and then restored me to life. His is the resurrection.[59]

Then make ready for the prayer. Having fulfilled all the conditions—the details of which have already been mentioned—turn towards the Ka'bah and perform the two voluntary *rak'ahs* of the dawn, of which the Prophet said, "The two dawn *rak'ahs* are better than this world and all that is in it.[60] "It is a confirmed Tradition that the Prophet observed these two *rak'ahs* even when he was travelling. After the two voluntary *rak'ahs*, perform the two obligatory *rak'ahs*, which might be prolonged by the recitation, aloud, of passages from the Qur'an. Through this prayer one may feel the glory of Islam and enjoy with the coming of the dawn the sweetness of the Qur'an:

The dawn recital carries their testimony.

(*Surah* al-'Isra', The Night Journey, 17:78)

Greet the new day with mercy and praise, beginning with a recitation from the Qur'an which will illuminate your soul. It will shine in the divine light of the tender dawn which is filled with everlasting mercy.

How the two rak'ahs are performed

We have already described in detail how to perform the first rak'ah.[61]

At the end of the second prostration of the first rak'ah, stand up and say:

بسم الله الرحمن الرحيم

In the name of Allah, the Compassionate, the Merciful.

Then recite the Opening Verse and a further short part of the Qur'an, and follow this with the bow and prostrations which you performed in the first rak'ah. At the end of the second prostration, remain seated on your left foot. While sitting in this position your left foot is laid flat on the ground and the right foot remains upright with the tips of the toes pointed towards the Ka'bah. Place your right hand on your right knee with the fingers together except for the index finger and thumb, which remain outspread. Placing your left hand on your left knee, recite the Profession of Faith and ask for the blessing of the Prophet, saying:

«التَّحيَّاتُ لله والصَّلَواتُ والطَّيِّباتُ . السَّلامُ عَلَيْكَ أَيُّها النَّبيُّ ورَحْمَةُ اللهِ وبرَكاتُهُ . السَّلامُ علَينا وعلى عِبادِ اللهِ الصَّالحين أَشْهَدُ أَنْ لا إله إلا اللهُ وأَشْهَدُ أَنَّ مُحمَّداً عَبْدُهُ ورسُولُهُ» .

Greetings, prayers, and the good things of life belong to Allah. The peace, mercy and blessing of Allah be upon you, O Prophet. Peace be upon us and on the devout servants of Allah. I bear witness that there is no deity save Allah[62] and I bear witness that Muhammad is His servant and Messenger.[63]

«اللَّهُـمَّ صلِّ على محمــد وعلى آل محمــد كمــا صليــت على إبراهيــم وعلَي آل إبراهيــم ، وبارك على محمد وعلى آل محمد كمـا بـاركـت على إبراهيم وعلــى آل إبراهيــم في العالمــين إنـك حميد مجيد» .

O Lord, bless Muhammad and his family as You blessed Abraham and his family. Give Your blessings to Muhammad and his family as You gave Your blessings to Abraham and his family in the world. You are the most praised, the most wonderful. [64]

These two verses together are known as "Words of Greeting."

After this, it is permissible for the worshipper to make those personal supplications which obtain for him the good things of this world and of the next. Indeed, this is the very time which is recommended for personal prayer, whether the prayer be Traditional or not. However, the Traditional prayers are preferable and the following prayers which, according to Ali ibn Abi Talib the Prophet used to say after the last "Words of Witness" and before the "Words of Peace" with which the ritual prayer ends:

١ـ «اللهم اغفر لي ما قدمت وما أخرت وما أسررت وما أعلنت وما أسرفت ، وما أنت أعلم به مني ، أنت المقدِّم وأنت المؤخر لا إله إلا أنت » .

Oh Lord, forgive me for what I have done and what I have not done; for what I have kept secret and what I have done openly; for my excess and that for which You know more than I do. You provide and You take away. There is no deity save You.[65]

According to Abdullah ibn Amr, Abu Bakr said to the Prophet, "Teach me a personal prayer that I may say during the ritual prayer." The Prophet said:

٢ـ «اللهم إني ظلمت نفسي ظلمًا كثيرًا ولا يغفر الذنوب إلا أنت فاغفر لي مغفرة من عندك وارحمني إنك أنت الغفور الرحيم» .

*O Lord, I have done great wrong. Only You can forgive sins. Grant me forgiveness and mercy. You are the All-Merciful, the All-Forgiving.*⁶⁶

٣ـ اللهم إني أعوذ بك من البخل والكسل وأرذل العمر وعذاب القبر وفتنة المحيا والممات .

*O Lord, I seek Your protection from meanness, from laziness, from a base life, from the torment of the grave, and from the trial of living and dying.*⁶⁷

After the words of Peace, first turn your head to the right, saying:

السلام عليكم ورحمة الله

The peace and mercy of Allah be upon you.

Then turn your head to the left, saying:

السلام عليكم ورحمة الله

The peace and mercy of Allah be upon you.

Although this concludes the prayer, it has been related that the Prophet, after saying, the Words of Peace twice, would say a personal prayer. It is therefore traditi that the believer memorize this prayer and, taking great Messenger as an example, also say the personal prayers.

There are a number of accounts of what the Prophet used to say.

1. According to Thawban, when the Messenger of Allah, had finished his prayer, he asked Allah's forgiveness three times, saying:

١ـ اَللّٰهُمَّ أَنْتَ السَّلامُ وَمِنْكَ السَّلامُ ، تَبَارَكْتَ يَا ذَا الجَلالِ وَالإِكرامِ .

O Allah, You are peace and peace comes from You. Blessed be the possessor of Majesty and Reverence.[68]

2. It is related by Abd al-Rahman ibn Ghanam that the Prophet said:

٢ـ عن عبد الرحمٰن بن غنْم أن النبي ﷺ قال : « مَنْ قَالَ قَبْلَ أَنْ يَنْصَرِفَ وَيَثْنِي رِجْلَهُ مِنْ صَلاةِ المَغْرِبِ وَالصُّبْحِ : لا إلهَ إلا اللهُ وَحْدَهُ لا شَرِيكَ لَهُ ، لَهُ المُلْكُ وَلَهُ الحَمْدُ بِيَدِهِ الخَيْرُ يُحْيِي وَيُمِيتُ وَهُوَ عَلَى كُلِّ شَيْءٍ قَدِيرٌ ، عَشْرَ مَرَّاتٍ ،

كُتب له بكل واحدة عشرُ صدقاتٍ ومُحيت عنه عشرُ سيئاتٍ ورُفع له عشرُ درجاتٍ وكانت حرزاً من كل مكروهٍ وحرزاً من الشيطان الرجيم، ولَم يحلّ لذنبٍ يُدركُه إلا الشرك . فكان مِن أفضلِ الناس عملاً إلا رجلاً يفضلُهُ يقولُ أفضل ممّا قال » .

Whosoever says before turning away from the evening and morning prayers,

There is no deity save Allah, He is One. He has no partner, His is the dominion and His is the praise. In His hand is prosperity. He brings life and death. He has power over all things';

Whoever says this ten times, to him is it ordained that each time a sin shall he wiped out; he will be raised ten ranks. It will be a talisman against all adversity, a talisman against the accursed Satan. No sin will consume him but that of Polytheism. He will become the finest of men in his deeds, being bettered only by one who says anything better than he himself has said.[69]

3. Al-Mughira ibn Shu'ba related that the Prophet used to say at the end of every obligatory prayer:

وعن المغيرة بن شعبة : أنَّ النبي ﷺ كان يقول دُبُرَ كلِّ صلاةٍ مكتوبةٍ : لا إله إلا الله وحدَهُ لا شريكَ لَهُ ، له الملك وله الحمدُ ، وهو على كُلِّ شيءٍ قدير اللهم لا مانعَ لما أعطيت ولا مُعطي لما منعتَ ، ولا ينفعُ ذا الجدِّ منك الجدُّ .

There is no deity save Allah, He is One. He has no partner. His is the dominion and His is the praise. He has power over all things. O Lord, none may withhold what You have given and none may give what You have withheld. His fortune will in no way serve the rich man in your eyes.[70]

At the end of each prayer, the Prophet used to recite the verse of the throne which is as follows:[71]

﴿ ٱللَّهُ لَآ إِلَٰهَ إِلَّا هُوَ ٱلۡحَيُّ ٱلۡقَيُّومُۚ لَا تَأۡخُذُهُۥ سِنَةٞ وَلَا نَوۡمٞۚ لَّهُۥ مَا فِي ٱلسَّمَٰوَٰتِ وَمَا فِي ٱلۡأَرۡضِۗ مَن ذَا ٱلَّذِي يَشۡفَعُ عِندَهُۥٓ إِلَّا بِإِذۡنِهِۦۚ يَعۡلَمُ مَا بَيۡنَ أَيۡدِيهِمۡ وَمَا خَلۡفَهُمۡۖ وَلَا يُحِيطُونَ بِشَيۡءٖ مِّنۡ عِلۡمِهِۦٓ إِلَّا بِمَا شَآءَۚ وَسِعَ كُرۡسِيُّهُ ٱلسَّمَٰوَٰتِ وَٱلۡأَرۡضَۖ وَلَا يَـُٔودُهُۥ حِفۡظُهُمَاۚ وَهُوَ ٱلۡعَلِيُّ ٱلۡعَظِيمُ ۝ ﴾ [البقرة]

Allah; there is no deity save Him, the Living, Self-sustaining the Eternal. No slumber can seize Him, nor sleep. His are all things in the heavens and on earth. Who is there who can intercede in His presence, except as He permits? He knows what (appears) to His creatures before or after or behind them. Nor shall they bypass any part of His knowledge, except as He wills. His throne extends over the heavens and the earth, and He feels no fatigue in guarding and preserving them, for He is the Most High, the Supreme.
(*Surah al-Baqarah*, The Heifer, 2:255)

You should memorize this passage of the Quran and recite it immediately after each prayer. Whoever recites it after his prayer is in Allah's protection until the next prayer.[72]

The Prophet used to recite the chapter of the Qur'an which begins, "I seek refuge..." and which is entitled, *Surah al-Falaq*, or "Day break" and *Surah an-Nas*, or "Humankind," immediately after the prayers. To these he added the *Surah al-Ikhlas*, or "Oneness."[73]

He also used to say.

O Lord, preserve me from the fire.[74]

HELP US!

Lord, give us what is good both in this world and in the next and save us from the chastisement of the Fire.

(*Surah al-Baqarah*, The Heifer, 2:201).

Lord, fill our hearts with steadfastness. Make firm our step and help us against the unbelievers.

(*Surah al-Baqarah*, The Heifer, 2:250).

Lord, do not cause our hearts to go astray after You have guided us. Grant us Your Own mercy; You are the Munificent Giver.

(*Surah al-Imran*, The Family of Imran, 3:8).

Lord, we believe in You: forgive us our sins and keep us from the torment of Hell-fire.

(*Surah al-e-Imran*, The Family of Imran, 3:16).

He would say these words seven times immediately after the morning prayer and likewise after the sunset prayer before speaking to anyone. To this he used to add, seven times, the following words:

اللهم إني أسألك الجنة.

O Lord, I ask you for paradise.[75]

Apart from this, the Prophet used to say the Words of Glory (Glory be to Allah), الحمد لله the "Words of Praise" (Praise be to Allah), الله أكبر and the Words of Greatness (Allah is Great), each thirty-three times, and to make the total up to a hundred, he would add:

لا إله إلا الله وحْـدهُ لا شَــريكَ لَهُ ، له المُلكُ وله الحَــمْــدُ وهُوَ على كلِّ شَيءٍ قَدير

There is no deity save Allah, He is One. He has no partner. His is the dominion and His the praise. He has power over all things.[76]

He would run them all together, saying:

ويجمعهن بقوله : اللهُ أكْبَرْ وَسُبْحانَ اللهِ والحمدُ للهِ .
اللهُ أكْبَرْ وَسُبْحانَ اللهِ والحمدُ للهِ .

Allah is great, glory be to Allah, praise be to Allah, Allah is Great, glory be to Allah, praise be to Allah, and so on, until he had said each phrase thirty-three times.[77]

In this manner the Prophet brought his prayer to an end, saying the words of peace, glory, greatness, and praise; seeking His forgiveness and making personal supplication to Him. His tongue was always moist with the constant mention of the name of Allah, whether he was standing, sitting, or lying on his side. He would meditate on the creation of heavens and earth. Each thought was a lesson, each silence a thought, and every word a mention of Allah.

It is fitting that we should do as the Prophet did; say a personal prayer when he did; and emulate him in his virtuous habits, word for word:

﴿ لَقَدْ كَانَ لَكُمْ فِي رَسُولِ ٱللَّهِ أُسْوَةٌ حَسَنَةٌ لِّمَن كَانَ يَرْجُواْ ٱللَّهَ وَٱلْيَوْمَ ٱلْآخِرَ وَذَكَرَ ٱللَّهَ كَثِيرًا ۝ ﴾ [الأحزاب]

You have indeed in the Apostle of Allah a beautiful pattern for anyone whose hope is in Allah and the Final Day and who engages much in the praise of Allah.

(*Surah al-Ahzab*, The Confederates, 33:21)

THE NOON PRAYER (ZUHR)

When the day is half done a man, stricken with fatigue and weary from work, seeks spiritual relief. It is at this time that he performs the noon prayer, which helps to restore his bodily vigour. He then turns towards the Ka'bah and is alone with his Lord. In spiritual communication with his Maker, he forgets his labour and his spiritual vigour is restored. Upon leaving the prayer, his lassitude will have been shaken off and he will return to his work with renewed vigour and determination.

The noon prayer has four traditional *rak'ahs* that precede the obligatory prayer. According to one confirmed Tradition, two traditional *rak'ahs* are performed before the obligatory prayer (which has four *rak'ahs*) and two after it. The recitation during the whole of the noon prayer is said to oneself, not aloud, whether one is leading the prayer, being led in prayer, or is alone.

How to perform the four *rak'ahs*

We have described in detail the morning prayer, which consists of two *rak'ahs*. If you know it well, it will be easy for you to perform all the prayers. When the prayer consists of four *rak'ahs*, it is the noon, afternoon, or sunset prayer.

When you have performed the first two *rak'ahs*, sit back and recite the "Profession of Faith" for the first time. After you are seated, recite the "Words of Greeting" as far as the "Profession of Faith," that is:

«التَحيّـاتُ لله والصَّـلواتُ والطَّيِّبَاتُ ، السَّــلامُ عَليْكَ أيُّها النَّبي ورحْمَةُ اللهِ وبَــركاتُهُ ، السَّــلامُ عَليْنا وعلى عبادِ اللهِ الصَّالحين ، أَشْهَدُ أَنَ لا إِله إِلا اللهُ وأَشْهَدُ أَنَّ مُحمَّداً عَبْدُهُ وَرَسَوْلُهُ» .

Greetings, prayers, and the good things of life belong to Allah. The peace, mercy, and blessing of Allah be upon you, O Prophet. Peace be upon us and on the devout slaves of Allah. I bear witness that there is no deity save Allah and I bear witness that Muhammad is His servant and Messenger.[78]

After this rise to your feet, place the right hand over the left and continue the prayers, performing the third and then the fourth *rak'ah*, during which you should recite only the Opening of the Qur'an: *Surah al-Faitha*. At the end of the fourth *rak'ah*, sit back and recite the first and last parts of the "Words of Witness", then say your personal prayer, and end with the "Words of Peace." The obligatory prayers are followed by two traditional *rak'ahs,* and with these the noon prayer is complete.

If you arrive at the mosque and see that the prayer has begun and that the *imam* is praying with the people, do not perform any voluntary prayers but join the congregation and follow the *imam*. The Messenger of Allah said: "Once the prayers are being performed, no prayers except the obligatory prayers are permitted."[79]

This applies to all prayers and is not specifically for one time rather than another. According to the command of the Prophet, you must follow the *imam*, even if you know that there is sufficient time for the voluntary prayers and that you can then catch up with him.

THE AFTERNOON PRAYER ('ASR)

The Quran says of the 'asr prayers:

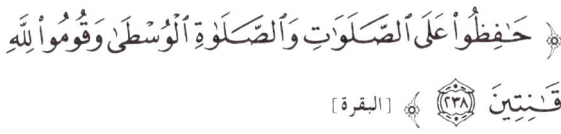

Attend strictly to your prayers, especially the Middle Prayer, and stand before Allah with all devotion.

(*Surah al-Baqarah,* The Heifer, 2:238)

According to most authorities, the "middle prayer" is the afternoon prayer. It consists of four obligatory *rak'ahs*, which are carried out exactly as the four *rak'ahs* of the noon prayer. During the first two *rak'ahs*, recite the Opening Verse of the Qur'an and another chapter with it, then sit back for the first "Profession of Faith." In the second two *rak'ahs*, recite only the Opening Verse of the Qur'an, and at the end of the fourth *rak'ah*, sit back for the final "Profession of Faith," concluding with the "Words of Peace."

The performance of voluntary prayers in the afternoon is not a confirmed tradition, however, there are four[80] voluntary *rak'ahs* to be carried out before the obligatory ones, although this is not supported by tradition either. Two *rak'ahs* may also be performed.[81]

Recitation during the afternoon prayers is performed silently to oneself throughout all the *rak'ahs*. Until the time comes for the sunset prayer, saying prayers after the afternoon prayers is to be avoided.

THE SUNSET PRAYER (MAGHRIB)

The Muslim starts the day with mercy (prayers are mercy), praising and glorifying Almighty Allah, and ends his day with mercy and gratitude, prayers to his Lord, who changes night into day, day into night and one thing into another.

There are three obligatory *rak'ahs* in the sunset prayer. The first two *rak'ahs* are performed by reciting them aloud, after which one sits back for the first "Profession of Faith." Then rise to your feet and perform the third *rak'ah*, reciting to

PROTECT US!

Lord, give us joy in our spouses and offspring, and cause us to be foremost among those who are God-fearing.

(Surah al-Farqan, 25:74).

Inspire me, Lord, to render thanks for the favours You have bestowed on me and on my parents, and to do good work that will please You. Admit me, through Your mercy, among your righteous servants.

(Surah al-Naml, The Ant, 27:19).

Lord, Your mercy and knowledge embrace all things. Forgive those that repent and follow Your path. Shield them from the scourge of Hell. Admit them, Lord, to the Gardens of Eden which You have promised them, together with all the righteous among their fathers, their spouses, and their descendents. You are the Almighty, the Wise One. Deliver them from all evil. He whom You will deliver from evil on that Day is surely one You have graced with Your mercy. That is the supreme triumph.

(Surah Ghafir, The Forgiving One, 40:7-9).

yourself only the Opening Verse of the Qur'an. After the second prostration of this *rak'ah*, sit back for the last "Profession of Faith," and recite the whole of the "Words of Greeting." After personal prayers, the obligatory prayer concludes with the "Words of Peace." Following the obligatory prayers are two voluntary *rak'ahs*, which are a confirmed tradition.

These two *raka's* complete the sunset prayer.

All the sunnah (traditional) *rak'ahs* are performed not by reciting them aloud, but by saying them to oneself. Reciting aloud only takes place during the two obligatory *rak'ahs* of the morning prayer and the first two obligatory *rak'ahs* of the sunset and evening prayers. During the remainder of the obligatory *rak'ahs*, recitation is to oneself.

THE EVENING PRAYER ('ISHA')

This consists of four obligatory *rak'ahs*, which are performed in the same way as are the four *rak'ahs* of the noon prayer, except that the recitation in the first two *rak'ahs* is done aloud. The obligatory *rak'ahs* are followed by two voluntary *rak'ahs*, these latter in accordance with confirmed traditional practice. Before the obligatory *rak'ahs*, it is permissible to perform two or four voluntary *rak'ahs*. These prayers are brought to an end by the separate Prayer *(witr)*.

THE WITR PRAYER

The meaning of the Arabic name for this prayer is "an odd number" and is the name given to the single *rak'a*h which is separated from all that have gone before. It may also consist of three, five, or seven *rak'ahs* all linked together, as in the obligatory *rak'ahs* of the sunset prayers. It is a name given to three *rak'ahs* linked together.

The *witr* Prayer is a confirmed traditional practice and is, indeed, the best attested of the traditions. According to some Imams it has the force of obligation.

The minimum number of *rak'ahs* in the *witr* prayer is one and the maximum is thirteen. The best number is three and is preferred by most Muslims today. The author of *Al-Musawat* says: "In the view of most people, the minimum number of *rak'ahs* in the *witr* prayer is one and the maximum is eleven or thirteen. The nearest to perfection is three, but to exceed that number is better.

The Prophet used to perform three *rak'ahs*. During the first he would recite, after the Opening Verse,

The Most High[82]

In the second,

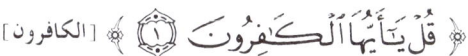

The Unbeliever[83]

and in the third,

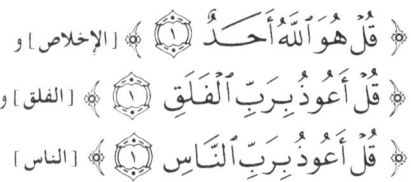

"Unity, Daybreak, and Men."[84]

The time for the *witr* prayer is from the end of the evening prayer until daybreak, and this is the last prayer of the night. Since this is so, and in order that its performance should not be a burden, many ways, all of them correct, have been related for performing it:

The three *rak'ahs* are all linked together, therefore, you do not sit back except after the third in which the whole of the "Words of Greeting" are recited, followed by the "Words of Peace." This method prevents it from being like the sunset prayer. The Prophet forbade that the *witr* prayers should resemble the sunset prayer.[85]

Perform two *rak'ahs* and round them off with the "Words of Peace ." Then perform a single *rak'a,* thus completing your prayer.

By this method the three *rak'ahs* are not separated by the "W   Peace," but rather by sitting back after the first
              hen by saying at the third the "Words of
              hen bowing. In each *rak'ah* the Opening Verse
              passage are recited.

If one wishes to say the "Words of Obedience," first recite the "Words of Greatness" and then raise the hands. Either of the following two prayers are recited:

١ـ «اَللّهُمَّ إِنَّا نَسْتَعِينُكَ ، وَنَسْتَغْفِرُكَ ، وَنَسْتَهْدِيكَ ، وَنُؤمِنُ بِكَ ، وَنَتُوبُ إِلَيْكَ ، وَنَتوكَّلُ عَلَيْكَ ، وَنُثْنِي عَلَيْكَ الخَيْرَ كُلَّهُ ، نَشْكُرُكَ وَلا نَكْفُرُكَ ، وَنَخْلَعُ وَنَتْرُكُ مَنْ يَفْجُرُكَ . اَللّهُمَّ إِيَّاكَ نَعْبُدُ ، وَلَكَ نُصَلِّي وَنَسْجُدُ ، وَإِلَيْكَ نَسْعَى وَنحفدُ ، نَرْجُــو رَحْمَتَكَ ، وَنَخْشَــى عَذَابَكَ ، إِنَّ عَذَابَكَ الجدَّ بالكفــار مُلْحِقٌ» (ويُقرأ مُلْحَقٌ بالفتح أيضاً) .

O Lord, we seek help from You, we seek[86] *Your forgiveness, we seek Your guidance, we turn in repentance to You. We place our trust in You. We laud Your name. We give thanks to You for the prosperity You have bestowed. We do not turn from You in disbelief. We renounce and turn away from whoever disobeys You and breaks Your commandments.*

O Lord, we worship You. To You we pray and to You we kneel. To You we hasten, to work for You and to serve You. We beg for Your mercy and fear Your punishment. One on whom Your punishment falls is surely an unbeliever. Your punishment will overtake and strike the unbeliever.

٢- «اللّهُـمَّ اهْدِني فيمَنْ هَدَيْـتَ ، وعافِنـي في مَنْ عافَيْـتَ ، وتَوَلَّني فيمَنْ تَوَلَّيْتَ ، وبارِكْ لي فيما أَعْطَيْتَ ، وقِني شَرَّ ما قَضَيْـتَ ، فإِنَّك تَقْضـي ولا يُقْضـى عَلَيْك ، إِنَّه لا يَـذِلُّ مَنْ والَيْتَ ، ولا يَعِزُّ مَنْ عادَيْتَ ، تَبارَكْتَ رَبَّنا وتَعالَيْتَ .

O Lord, lead me to the true faith with those You have guided. Pardon me with those You have pardoned. Protect me with those You have protected. Bless me with what you have given. Keep me safe from the evil You have ordained, for You decree and none passes decrees upon You. No one who is in Your care is brought low and no one is rewarded to whom You show enmity. O Lord, You are most praised, most sublime.[87]

According to many Imams, the "Words of Obedience" (*qunut* قنوت) are not said except in the second half of Ramadan, but according to the Hanafis, they may be recited throughout the year. Others, including Imam Malik, hold that it is incorrect to say them at any time of the year.

TO THE LORD

Lord, do not take us to task if we forget or lapse into error. Lord, do not lay on us the burden You laid on those before us. Lord, do not charge us with more than we can bear. Pardon us, forgive us our sins, and have mercy upon us. You alone are our Protector. Give us victory over the deniers.

(*Surah al-Baqarah*, The Heifer, 2:286).

Allah, Lord of all sovereignty, You bestow sovereignty on whom You will and take it away from whom You please; You exalt whomever You will and abase whomever You please. In Your hand lies all that is good; You have power over all things. You cause the night to pass into the day and the day to pass into the night; You bring forth the living from the dead and the dead from the living. You give without stint to whom You will.

(*Surah al-e-Imran*, The Family of Imran, 3:26-27).

With the end of the *witr* prayer, the evening prayer and the five prayers are complete. In this way the Muslim spends his day and night in worship of, obedience to, and sincerity of purpose towards Allah, Lord of Heaven and Earth, and goes to sleep praying to Allah, exalting, praising and giving thanks to Him, just as he did when awoke in the morning.

SOME IMPORTANT NOTES

While you are performing the prayers, you must observe the proprieties and rules. You must not speak or look to your right or left, or move your limbs or body other than as custom requires. If you speak during prayer, or concern yourself with anything not connected with prayer, or deliberately break any of the rules, your prayer is invalid and you must do it again, this time fulfilling all the required conditions.

When you are performing the prayers, do not raise your eyes to heaven, and do not close them. Your eyes should be open. If you are standing, you should direct your gaze to the spot where you will be prostrating yourself. If you are bowing, you should direct your gaze to the top of your feet. When you sit back to say the "Words of Greeting," look at your right hand and the finger which will be raised during the "Profession of Faith."

You are permitted to perform the prayers wearing shoes. When this is done, you must first turn them over and look at the soles. Should you see any wetness or defilement, wipe it off on the ground. You may then perform the prayers in them. It is a traditional practice to perform the prayers wearing shoes, so as to be differentiated from the Jews.[88]

The whole world is a mosque and ritually pure, therefore, pray wherever you may be when the time for prayers arrives; but never in a cemetery, in the bathroom or where total ablution is carried out, for any prayers performed in these places are invalid.

If you have been eating garlic, onions, leeks, or anything similar, which has unpleasant odour, you should not enter the mosque[89], thereby causing annoyance to the worshippers, but rather wait until the odour has dissipated.

It is traditional to say on entering the mosque:

بِسْمِ اللهِ والصَّلاةِ والسَّلامُ عَلَى رَسُولِ اللهِ ، اللَّهُـمَّ اغْفِرْ لي ذُنُوبي ، وافْتَحْ لي أَبْوابَ رَحْمَتِكَ .

In the name of Allah. Peace be on the Messenger of Allah. O Lord, forgive me my sins and open to me the gates of Your mercy.[90]

You should step inside with the right foot first and leave with the left foot first, saying:

بِسْمِ اللهِ وَالصَّلاةُ وَالسَّلامُ عَلَى رَسُولِ اللهِ ، اللَّهُمَّ اغْفِرْ لِي ذُنُوبِي وَافْتَحْ لِي أَبْوابَ فَضْلِكَ .

In the name of Allah. Blessing and peace be on the Messenger of Allah. O Lord, forgive me my sins, and open to me the gates of your favour.[91]

Anyone performing the prayers may not allow any thoughts to enter his mind which are contrary to a state of humility. On the contrary, he must concern himself only with thoughts of Allah and his dependence on Him. If such a thought comes to him, his prayers are not made invalid, but he must put it out of his mind and return to humility, thinking of the Majesty of Allah before whom he is standing.

If, in the course of prayer, a snake or scorpion, etc., should pass by, then one is allowed to kill it.[92] This action will not invalidate the prayer.

If a small child should cling to you while you are performing the prayer, either put him to one side or carry him on your shoulder and continue the prayers.[93] If someone knocks on the door while you are performing the prayer, and there is no one else in the house, go to the door and open it.[94]

These simple movements will not invalidate the prayer.

A Muslim may not pass in front of anyone performing the prayers. The worshipper may place some sort of screen in front of him such as a pole, a tree, a wall, a chair, an upright stick, or he should draw a line[95] on the ground, if he is unable to do anything else. It is permissible to pass on the other side of this screen. If, however, anyone passes between this mark and the worshipper, the worshipper may gently push him aside.[96]

If some calamity befalls the individual or the community, such as an enemy attack or an epidemic, or some other emergency arises, then saying the "words of Obedience"[97] or *qunut*, during each of the five prayers becomes obligatory for the worshipper, whether he be alone or in a congregation, until the calamity has passed. Then the practice ceases.

The "Words of Obedience" are recited only during the last obligatory *rak'ah*. The worshipper raises his hands after rising from the last prostration and says a personal prayer for himself and his community, invoking Allah against the enemies of his people and country by any form of supplication that he wishes.

It is permitted to say the "Words of Praise" (*al hamdu lillahi* الحمد لله) during the prayers for a favour which has been granted or for a sneeze. If a worshipper should come upon a verse concerning punishment, tradition requires that he should seek refuge in Allah from it.[98] If he whould recite, for example:

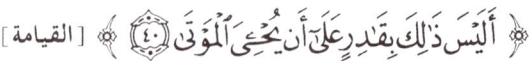

[القيامة]

Has not He the Power to give life to the dead?

(*Surah al-Qiyamah,* The Resurrection, 75:40)

or other verses which ask a question of this kind, he may then say, *bala*[99] (بـلـى) "Yes." If someone should say السلام عليكم "Peace be upon you" while you are performing the prayers, answer him with no more than a gesture.[100]

THE PROSTRATION OF FORGETFULNESS

Man is subject to forgetfulness, so if you should forget something while performing your prayers—either doing something which is not prescribed or leaving something out—you must carry out two prostrations, similar to those in the prayers, reciting the "Words of Greatness" while dropping to the ground and rising at the end of the "Words of Greeting." After this recite the "Words of Peace," but omitting the "Profession of Faith."

If you are in doubt during the performance of a prayer, as to whether you have completed one or two *rak'ahs,* you should regard it as one. If you are in doubt as to whether you have completed two or three, you should count them as two. And if you are in doubt as to whether you have completed three or four, you should count them as three. The *rak'ahs* about which you are in doubt should then be completed with the "Words of Peace" being recited either before[101] them or after[102] them. Either way was laid down by the Messenger of Allah.

If you forget to say the first "Profession of Faith," perform two *rak'ahs* and stand up for the third without sitting back. Complete the *prayers*, then make two further prostrations

SAVE US FROM EVIL

Lord, we have wronged our souls. Pardon us and have mercy on us, or we shall surely be among the lost.
(*Surah al-A'raf*, The Height, 7:23).

Lord, bless us with patience and let us die as Muslims (who have surrendered themselves to Your Will).
(*Surah al-A'raf*, The Height, 7:126).

Lord, You alone are our Guardian. Forgive us and have mercy on us: You are the Best of those who forgive. Ordain for us what is good, both in this life and in the Hereafter. To You alone we have turned in repentance.
(*Surah al-A'raf*, The Height, 7:155-156).

Lord, do not let us suffer at the hands of the wicked. Deliver us, through Your mercy, from the unbelievers.
(*Surah Yunus*, Jonah, 10:85-86).

Creator of the heavens and earth, You are my Guardian in this world and in the next. Let me die as one submitting to Your Will (i.e., Muslim) and join the righteous.

(*Surah Yusuf*, Joseph, 12:101).

before or after the "Words of Peace" of the last *rak'ah*. This atones for your act of forgetfulness.

If you are in the mosque awaiting the prayers, whether it be Friday or any other day, and you hear a reader of the Qur'an reciting a verse of prostraton, then perform a single Prostration of Recitation.

PERFORMANCE OF THE PRAYER BY ONE WHO IS SICK

If it is impossible for a sick person to stand, he should perform the prayers seated, bowing and prostrating himself from this position[103]. If he is unable to bow or prostrate himself, he should make a token gesture with his head, bringing it lower for a prostration than for a bow. If he is unable to sit, he should perform the prayers lying on his side, facing in the direction of the Ka'bah. If he is unable to do that, he should perform the prayers lying on his back with his legs pointing towards the Ka'bah and making token gestures for the bows and prostrations.[104]

Should he be unable to do even this, then the prayer is postponed. Such is the importance of prayer in Islam that you must perform it no matter what your condition. You may not ignore this duty even though you are sick. For this, glory be to Almighty Allah, the Only One.

CONGREGATIONAL PRAYER

Islam is the religion of unity and monotheism. It demands the acceptance of the Oneness of Almighty Allah, the existence of the one Word of Allah, and a close adherence to the strong bond which links us with Him. It also requires Muslims to assemble for prayers in the mosques, to get to know each other, and to treat each other with truth and patience. Islam considers congregational prayer to be twenty-seven times better than solitary prayer, which demonstrates how glorious and important is the act of praying together. Here are some of the Traditions of the Messenger of Allah regarding the superiority of praying together:

Ibn 'Umar relates that the Prophet said: "Praying together is twenty- seven times better than the individual praying alone."[105]

Abu al-Darda'a heard the Prophet say: "There were never three villagers or Pedouins who did not perform the prayers together and who were not over-powered by Satan. You must group together, for the wolf eats up the sheep which is away from the flock."[106]

Mu'adh Ibn Anas quotes the Messenger of Allah as saying: "It is nothing but abhorrence, nothing but disbelief, nothing but hypocrisy, for one to hear Allah's caller calling to prayers, and not to respond."[107]

Ibn Umm Maktum said to the Prophet: "O Messenger of Allah; I am blind and my house is far away. My guide is not suitable for me. Do I not have permission to pray at home?" "Can you hear the call?" she replied: "Yes." He said, "There is no excuse for you."[108]

In another version of this Tradition related by Ahmad and al-Tabrani, the conversation went:

"O Messenger of Allah, my house is a long way off and I have become blind, yet I hear the call."

The Messenger said: "If you hear the call you must answer it, even if you have to crawl and drag yourself over the ground."[109]

You will see from these sacred Traditions, brother Muslim,

the importance of congregational prayers which you must observe and which must not be avoided, even by a blind man. Treat it as a matter of conscience which must be observed. Recognise that it is a duty for all men of sound mind, unless they are excused because of sickness or fear of being placed in peril, or because it will bring about undue hardship or harm. This is the most important tradition in Islam.

Women are permitted to attend the congregation in the mosque and their husbands may not prevent them from doing so, unless it is feared that harm may come to them as a result of performing the prayers in the mosque rather than at home[110]. The reward for congregational prayers will be obtained, even though there are only two, one of whom is a child or a woman, although the greater the number, the better it is. Congregational prayer is the most glorious of Islamic religious practices, the greatest of religious acts, whereby the old and the young, the rich and the poor, the powerful and the wretched, all stand before Allah with no difference between them, all on an equal footing. The best of them are those who fear Allah. In congregational prayers, impartiality, equality, and obedience are very much in evidence, when the rich and the poor and the ruler and the subject stand in a single row, meeting in one place. Once Muslims know the meaning and significance of this, how can they ever abandon or neglect this practice? How can they complain to Allah that other Muslims have deserted them and kept away from them?

HOW THE CONGREGATIONAL PRAYER IS PERFORMED

If you are a member of a group and you all wish to perform the prayers, you should perform it together and not individually. The *Imam* should be the one among you who recites the Qur'an best, and if you are all equal in this respect, then the *Imam* should be the one who is most learned and most versed in the Traditions of the Messenger of Allah. Should you all be equal in these respects, then the oldest of you shall be appointed[111]. In the mosques, the *Imams* are well-known and they lead the prayers, but they must be chosen with care.

After the *Imam* is chosen, he goes forward to perform the prayers with you and stands in front of you in the centre of the row. Then he looks at the row in which the congregation is formed and straightens it out. (Straightening the row is one of the finer points of the ritual of the prayers).[113]

After the second call the *imam* says the "Words of Greatness" and performs the prayers. You say the "Words of Greatness" after him. A person who is being led in prayer does not follow the *Imam's* recitation of the Qur'an except for the Opening Verse. He follows the *Imam* in the movements of the prayers, bows after him, stands up from the bow after him, prostrates himself after him, and so on until the end of the prayer. The *Imam* says the "Words of Peace" and the congregation repeats them after Him. It is forbidden for a person being led in prayer to do anything before or even at the same time as the *Imam*.

The *Imam* recites aloud those parts of the prayers which are ritually recited aloud and recites the other parts to himself. But those who are led in prayers recite only the Opening Verse and that at all times to themselves.

Congregational prayers may be held with only two people, even though one of them is a child or a woman. If you wish to perform the prayers and there is only one other person with you, the one who is to be led stands to the right of the one who is leading but not behind him. If another person comes, to follow your example, the person being led should move backwards, the third person joining him, so as to form a row, with the *Imam* between them. If those who are following do not know the rule and form up on the right and left of the *Imam*, he should take them by the arm and gently push them back, so as to form a row behind him. If a person following the *Imam* is his wife or sister, she must stand behind the *imam* and not to his right. It is permissible for a boy to be chosen to lead the men in their obligatory prayers, provided he recites the Qur'an better than they, or if he is better versed in theology than they.

He who accomplishes one *rak'ah* with the *Imam* has attained the benefit of the congregational prayers. If he has omitted any part of the prayer with the *Imam*, he performs it after the *Imam* has said the "Words of Peace." So if you have missed anything, when the *Imam* completes the prayers and says the "Words of Peace," do not do so, but stand up and complete the *rak'ahs* which have been missed. It is required by tradition that the *Imam* shall be brief in performing the prayers, because the congregation includes those who are weak, or aged, or who have urgent physical needs.

DO NOT LEAVE ME ALONE!

Lord, put courage into my heart, and ease my task for me. Free my tongue from its impediment, so that they may understand my speech.

(Surah Ta Ha, 20:25-28).

Lord, cause me to grow in knowledge.

(Surah Ta Ha, 20:114).

Lord, I have been afflicted with distress: but You are the Most Merciful of all who show mercy.

(Surah al-Arbiya', The Prophets, 21:83).

Lord, do not leave me childless; You are the Best of all heirs.

(Surah al-Arbiya', The Prophets, 21:89).

Lord, let my landing from this ark be blessed. You alone can make me land in safety.

(Surah al-Mu'minun, The Believers, 23:29).

Lord, build me a house with You in Paradise.

(Surah at-Tahrim, Prohibition, 66:11).

Lord, I stand in need of the blessing which You have sent me.

(Surah al-Qasas, The Story, 28:24).

Lord, deliver me from these corrupt people.

(Surah al-'Akabut, The Spider, 29:30).

Avenge me, Lord, I am overcome!

(Surah al-Qamar, The Moon, 54:10).

Shortening of the prayers is done only in the lines recited after the "Opening Verse," and not in the bows, prostrations and elevations, which must be carried out without haste, for not performing them properly diminishes the prayers. The way in which some *imams* and some people rush through the prayers today, bobbing up and down like hens pecking at the ground, is unlawful and renders the prayers void. If the prayer is divested of humility, it is invalid and the goal which worshippers hoped to achieve is thereby missed.

It not permitted for a man to perform the prayers standing alone behind a row. If he comes to perform the prayer and finds the row full and can find no place in which to enter it. he must gently draw[113] a man from the last row to stand with him and together form a last row. The prayer of anyone who prays alone behind the *imam* is void.

It is not permitted for a person spoken of as immoral or ignorant, or who is disliked by the God-fearing, to lead the people in prayers. Such a person should stand apart to permit someone who is more knowledgeable, upright, and God-fearing to come forward. Only a person who is worthy may be appointed as *imam*, for the *imams* are our earthly link with our Lord.

Ibn Umar tells us that Allah's Messenger said: "Let your *imams* be the best among you, for they are your representatives between you and your Lord."[114] And Al-Hakim quotes the Prophet as saying: "If you wish to be made happy by having your prayers accepted, then your *imams* should be the best among you, for they are your representatives between you and your Lord."[115]

PRAYER DURING A JOURNEY

﴿ يُرِيدُ ٱللَّهُ بِكُمُ ٱلْيُسْرَ وَلَا يُرِيدُ بِكُمُ ٱلْعُسْرَ وَلِتُكْمِلُوا۟ ٱلْعِدَّةَ وَلِتُكَبِّرُوا۟ ٱللَّهَ عَلَىٰ مَا هَدَىٰكُمْ وَلَعَلَّكُمْ تَشْكُرُونَ ۝ ﴾ [البقرة]

Allah desires your well-being, not your discomfort. He desires you to fast the whole month so that you may glorify Him and render thanks to Him for giving you His guidance.

(*Surah al-Baqarah*, The Heifer, 2:185)

Islam is always like this. Allah does not impose discomfort upon anyone, nor does He give commands unless they are capable of being carried out. Because of the hardships which have to be endured during a journey, Allah has permitted that four *rak'ahs* be reduced to two. Some of the genuine Traditions hold that the prayers which require two *rak'ahs* shall be of two *rak'ahs*. This has become established for a journey, but the number of *rak'ahs* is increased again when the journey is over.[116] Therefore, if you are travelling, shorten the noon prayer to two *rak'ahs* instead of four and likewise the afternoon and evening prayers. But the sunset and morning prayers remain as they are and are not shortened.

The voluntary and traditional prayers may be shortened to two *rak'ahs* only for the morning prayer and the *witr* prayer. Shortening the prayers is a dispensation and gift from Allah to the worshippers who fear Him and they must accept the gift, for Allah "wants you to accept His gifts as he wants you to accept His adjurations."[117] You are therefore required to shorten the prayers while travelling and this is an obligatory duty. It makes no difference whether you go by air, by car, by ship, by train, by camel or on foot. All constitute travelling, and in all of them the prayers are shortened without distinction as to the mode of travel.

Shortening of the prayers lasts for as long as the worshipper is travelling. When he takes up residence in a country, he should then complete the prayers with four *rak'ahs*, but there are various views as to what constitutes a period of residence, during which time the prayers are performed in full. The Imam Al-Shafi'i stated: "If he intends to stay in place for four days, his sojourn should not properly be reckoned (as part of a term of residence)." Abu Hanifa was of the view that "he continues to be a traveller unless he intends to stay in a town or village for fifteen days or more."

According to others, he may use the shortened form of the prayers all the time, unless he decides to stay permanently.

During the war with the Hawazin, in the year of the conquest of Makkah, the Prophet shortened his prayers for eighteen or nineteen days.[118] If a man arrives at a town, but does not intend to stay in it for any specific period, saying, "I will leave tomorrow or the day after," then delays his departure because its not convenient to leave, his prayers continues to be shortened, even though this state of affairs may continue for years. If a man returns to his own country from a journey, he performs the prayers in full, even though he does not intend to stay there. If a person should miss a prayer during a journey, he performs two *rak'ahs* in his residence. For example, if a person from Baghdad was in Egypt when the time for the noon prayer arrived, but he was unable to perform it because of his preoccupation with his journey, then he boarded an airplane to Baghdad which he reached after the afternoon prayer, he would perform two *rak'ahs* for the noon prayer. The reverse applies also, in that a person missing the prayers in his residence must perform four *rak'ahs* on his journey.

There are differing views as to what should be the period of the journey before the rules apply. Some say it should be three days and nights by camel or on foot and others say differently. The opinion of the scholars in Tradition is that there is nothing which specifies the length of the journey during which the traveller shortens the prayers. One must refer to what is defined as a journey in language and in law. The Quran says:

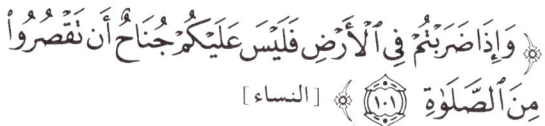

When travelling the road, there is no blame on you if you shorten your prayers.

(*Surah al-Nisa*, The Woman, 4:101).

"Travelling the road" holds true for every journey except for going for a walk, or a picnic, during which the prayers are not shortened. The tradition of Shu'ba is related by Yahya Ibn Yazid Al-Huona'i:

"I asked Anas about shortening the prayers and he said, 'If the Messenger of Allah went three miles[119] or three parasangs,[120] he used to perform the prayers with two rak'ahs'"[121]

The traveller may not shorten the prayers until he has left the town with its suburbs and gardens completely behind him. A traveller may perform the prayers as the *Imam* for the residents of any place through which he is travelling, in which case he performs two *rak'ahs* followed by the "Words of Peace," the residents completing the full prayers by themselves. It is desirable that such an *Imam* should say to the residents, after saying the "Words of Peace;"

أتموا صلاتكم فإنا قوم سفر

Complete your prayer, for I am a traveller.[122]

It is also permitted for a traveller to perform the prayers behind a resident, following his example. He may shorten the[123] prayer or carry it out in full, as is done by the *Imam* and the congregation. It is better to perform the prayers in full because of what has been previously established in the Musnad of Ahmad as related by Ibn 'Abbas. He was asked "Why should the traveller perform two *rak'ahs* if he is alone and four if he is with the *Imam*?" He answered, "That is the tradition."[124]

Ibn 'Umar, as related by Muslim, said, "If I am with the *Imam*, I perform four *rak'ahs*. If I am praying alone, I perform two."[125]

JOINING PRAYERS TOGETHER

A traveller may perform two prayers without any interval between them. He may, for example, join the noon prayer and the afternoon prayer, delaying the noon prayer until the time comes for the afternoon prayer and performing both of them together at the latter time. Each prayer remains separate from the other, In this example, the afternoon prayer would be performed first, followed by the noon prayer. The worshipper makes only one first call for both prayer, but makes separate second calls for each prayers. This is called the joining of lateness. In the joining in advance, the afternoon prayer might be joined to the noon prayer and performed at noon or the evening prayer might be brought forward to the time of the sunset prayer. There is disagreement between the religious jurists regarding the latter type of joining, but the correct ruling is that it is permitted. Both types of joining are permitted when there is need for them.

Imam Ahmad and others relate the Tradition that at the time of the raid on Tabuk, if the Prophet was starting out before the sun began to decline from its zenith, he used to postpone the noon prayer until the afternoon prayer and perform them both together. If he was starting out after the sun began to decline, he would perform the noon prayer and the afternoon prayer together and then go.[126]

Imam Ahmad quotes Ibn Abbas to the same effect and adds to it the joining of the sunset prayer and the night prayer.[127]

The only prayers which may be joined are the noon and afternoon or the sunset and night prayers. Joining the morning and the noon prayers, for example, or the sunset and the afternoon prayers is not allowed. Joining is restricted to those prayers which consist of four *rak'ahs*, and was so ordained to relieve the lot of the people.

THE FRIDAY PRAYER

Islam is a great social religion. It fosters unity and demands that people meet. It abhors and shuns disunion, Not only does it give Muslims every opportunity to get to know each other and to be on intimate terms with each other, but indeed commands that they should avail of such opportunities.

Friday is a glorious day in Islam. It is the finest day on which the sun rises and is a feast day for Muslims. It is the day on which they remember Allah and glorify Him. In this great weekly meeting they gather in mosques leaving aside all worldly affairs, in order to carry out their religious obligations, to listen to the sermons of the preachers, and to receive spiritual guidance from the learned.

GRANT US A RIGHTEOUS END

Lord, You have not created this in vain. Glory be to You! Save us from the torment of Hell-fire. Lord, those whom You will cast into Hell shall be put to eternal shame: none will help the wrongdoers. Lord, we have heard a crier calling men to the true Faith, saying: "Believe in your Lord." So we believed. Lord, then, forgive us our sins and remove from us our evil deeds and make us die with the righteous. Lord, grant us what You promised through your Messengers, and do not cast shame on us on the Day of Resurrection. Truely, You never fail to fulfil Your promise.

(*Surah al-Imran,* The Family of Imran, 3:191-194).

The Friday sermon is a lesson in which the preachers deal with the daily problems of society. New problems constantly appear which demand that Muslims be enlightened by the torch of Islam. These problems affect every facet of their lives. In this way those who are closely tied to their religion retain their renown and distinction and remain so as long as they are pious and God-fearing.

Performance of the Friday prayers is one of the obligations imposed by Allah, as is made clear in the Qur'an:

﴿ يَا أَيُّهَا الَّذِينَ آمَنُوا إِذَا نُودِيَ لِلصَّلَاةِ مِن يَوْمِ الْجُمُعَةِ فَاسْعَوْا إِلَىٰ ذِكْرِ اللَّهِ وَذَرُوا الْبَيْعَ ۚ ذَٰلِكُمْ خَيْرٌ لَّكُمْ إِن كُنتُمْ تَعْلَمُونَ ۝ فَإِذَا قُضِيَتِ الصَّلَاةُ فَانتَشِرُوا فِي الْأَرْضِ وَابْتَغُوا مِن فَضْلِ اللَّهِ وَاذْكُرُوا اللَّهَ كَثِيرًا لَّعَلَّكُمْ تُفْلِحُونَ ۝ ﴾ [الجمعة]

Believers, when the call is proclaimed to prayers on Friday, hasten earnestly to the remembrance of Allah, and leave off business. That is best for you if you but knew it, and when the prayers are finished, you may disperse and go your ways in quest of the bounty of Allah, and celebrate the praise of Allah often, so that you may prosper.

(*Surah al-Jumua*, The Congregation, 62:9-10)

Friday prayer is obligatory for every adult Muslim who is in residence. It applies to every group of people who live together, even though they live in the smallest hamlet.

Many sayings of the Messenger of Allah on the Friday prayer have come down to us such as, "He who stays away from it should be consumed by fire."[128] The Prophet himself performed the duty regularly from the time Allah ordained it until his death.[129] Forbidding the abandonment of the practice, he said from his pulpit:

"Let people desist and refrain from neglecting the Friday prayers, otherwise Allah will make their hearts inaccessible and they will be among those who are ignored."[130]

He also said:

"He who deliberately neglects three Friday prayers, will have a mark made on his heart by Allah."[131]

In his sermon on the day when the Friday prayer was made obligatory, he said:

"Let it be known that Allah has prescribed the Friday prayer for you on this spot, on this day, in this month, in this year, until the Day of Judgment. Whoever neglects it during or after my lifetime, even though he has an *imam* who is neglectful and strays from the right path, who disdains and rejects Allah's ordinance, may Allah grant him no reunification. Neither will his affairs be blessed. There shall be no prayers for him, no almsgiving, no pilgrimage, no fast. There will be no righteousness in him until he repents. Allah will restore His grace and favour to whoever repents to Him."[132]

How to perform the Friday prayer

The Friday prayer is only permissible in the mosques in which Muslims congregate and where their *Imam* preaches to them, giving them advice and spiritual guidance. The time for the Friday prayer is the time of the noon prayer, although some have it that it is permitted before the sun has reached its zenith. It is required by Tradition that on Friday you should bathe and perform the total ablution, that you should put on sweet smelling perfumes, and wear your best and cleanest clothes, then in a calm and dignified manner should go to the mosque.

On entering the mosque one should say:

"O Lord, open to me the gates of Your mercy."[133] Before you sit down to await the prayer, perform two *rak'ahs* as a traditional greeting to the mosque. The Prophet said, "When any one of you enters the mosque, do not sit until you have performed two *rak'ahs*."[134] After this be seated and listen to the recitation of the Qur'an, meditating on the meaning of the verses. If there is no one reciting the Qur'an, you can do no better than to sit down quietly, contemplating and remembering Allah. When the time comes to perform the prayers, the *muezzin* makes the call, the recitation ends; the worshippers arise and offer two or four[135] voluntary *rak'ahs* to Allah before the preacher mounts the pulpit. These *rak'ahs* on Friday are voluntary and are not required or confirmed by Tradition as some people think. Voluntary *rak'ahs* are desirable at all times, but while the Prophet used to encourage them on Fridays, it was not specified or demanded that they be performed. The learned men of Islam say that voluntary *rak'ahs* are permitted before the Friday prayer as long as the Imam has not appeared; but once he has appeared there must be no praying and no speaking.

At the end of the voluntary prayer, one observes the preacher going up to the pulpit.

In front of him the *muezzin* gives the call to Prayer and you answer him. You must then devote your whole attention to the sermon. You are forbidden to speak during the sermon, even though you only say "Shush!" to the person beside you, otherwise the prayer will be void. Whoever speaks has not performed the Friday prayer.[136]

When the two sermons are finished—which the preacher separates by sitting down between them—he comes down from the pulpit, the second call is made, and he performs the obligatory Friday prayers of two rak'ahs as the Imam, the congregation following him. The Friday prayer is exactly the same as the obligatory morning prayer, differing only in the intention. In the morning prayer you state your intention of performing the Morning Prayer, whereas on Friday you state your intention to perform the Friday Prayer.

At the end of the two *rak'ahs* the *imam* says the "Words of Peace" and the worshippers say them after him. After this the traditional Friday "following prayer" is performed. This may be done either in the mosque or upon your arrival at home. It consists of four *rak'ahs*. Tradition holds that the Prophet said, "If any one of you perform the Friday prayer, let him perform four *rak'ahs* after it."[137] It has also been related that it should be only two *rak'ahs*.[138]

The traditional *rak'ahs* of the "following prayer" complete the obligations, traditional requirements, and proprieties of the Friday. Afterwards people may go their own way in search of Allah's grace and favour. Almighty Allah said:

﴿ فَإِذَا قُضِيَتِ ٱلصَّلَوٰةُ فَٱنتَشِرُوا۟ فِى ٱلْأَرْضِ وَٱبْتَغُوا۟ مِن فَضْلِ ٱللَّهِ وَٱذْكُرُوا۟ ٱللَّهَ كَثِيرًا لَّعَلَّكُمْ تُفْلِحُونَ ۝ ﴾ [الجمعة]

And when the prayer is finished, you may disperse and go your ways in quest of the bounty of Allah, and celebrate the praise of Allah often, so that you may prosper.

(Surah al-Jumu'a, The Congregation, 62:10)

HAVE MERCY ON US!

Lord, make me and my descendents steadfast in prayer. Lord, accept my prayer. Forgive me, Lord, and forgive my parents and all the faithful on the Day of Reckoning.

(Surah Ibrahim, Abraham, 14:40-41).

Lord, have mercy on them both (i.e., my parents) as they cherished and cared for me when I was a little child.

(Surah al-Isra', The Night Journey, 17:24).

THE PRAYER OF THE TWO FEASTS

The prayer of *Id al-Fitr*, offered on the *Id* day which is celebrated after completion of the fasting of Ramadan, and the prayer of Id al-Adha, the Feast of sacrifice which is celebrated during the Hajj. Each of these prayers consists of two rak'ahs, during which the *imam* recites aloud. There is no Call to prayer and no Second Call. No prayers of any kind are said before or after them, and the time to perform them is from twenty minutes after sunrise until noon.

The prayer of the feast of the breaking of the fast (*Id al-Fitr*)

Following the obligatory fasting of the blessed month of Ramadan, Muslims celebrate with the *Id al-Fitr* which lasts for three days. They welcome this feast with personal prayers, and by giving praise to Almighty Allah.

After performing the Morning Prayer on the first day of Shawwal (شهر شوال) the worshipper goes to the mosque, having first carried out the total ablution,[139] dressed himself in his best clothes, purified and perfumed himself, and broken his fast, even though only with a few dates.[140] All these things follow the Tradition of the Prophet during the Feast. He enters the mosque, sits down without performing any prayers whatever, and listens to the recitation of the holy Qur'an[141] until the sun rises. When the sun has been up for twenty minutes and is clearly visible, that is the time for the prayers of the *Id al-Fitr*.

The *imam* stands up to perform this blessed prayer[142] with the people. The people stands in rows, which he straightens. He then says the "Words of Greatness" and the people say them after him. Then all recite the Opening verse. After this the *imam* says the "Words of Greatness" (الله أكبر) six times,[143] with the congregation repeating them after him, on each occasion raising his hands to his ears, then putting them together on his chest. The congregation follows suit. Between each recitation of the Words of Greatness, they all recite to themselves the words:

«سُبْحَانَ اللهِ، وَالحمدُ للهِ، وَلا إلهَ إلا اللهُ، واللهُ أكْبَرُ»

Glory be to Allah. Thanks be to Allah.
There is no deity save Allah.
Allah is Great. [144]

These "Words of Greatness," totalling seven in all, are completed before the recitation of the Qur'an begins. The *imam* then recites the Opening Verse aloud, and it is recommended that after it he should recite the whole of the chapter beginning ﴿ سَبِّحِ اسْمَ رَبِّكَ الْأَعْلَى ۝ ﴾ [الأعلى] "Glorify the Name of your Guardian Lord, the Most High."[145] after it. He then bows and makes two prostrations in the customary way five times, separating each by the words:

« سُبْحَانَ اللهِ، وَالْحَمْدُ لِلَّهِ، وَلَا إِلَهَ إِلَّا اللهُ، وَاللهُ أَكْبَرُ »

Glory be to Allah. Thanks be to Allah.
There is no deity save Allah.
Allah is Great.

He then recites the Opening Verse aloud, and it is recommended that he should recite the whole of the chapter beginning ﴿ هَلْ أَتَاكَ حَدِيثُ ٱلْغَاشِيَةِ ﴾ (Surah 101, al-Qari'ah, The Disaster)"[146]

After this the *imam* bows and prostrates himself, then sits back to say the "Profession of Faith" and recite the "Words of Greeting." He concludes the prayer with the "Words of Peace" followed by the "Words of Greatness" in which he is joined by the congregation saying:

«الله أكبر ، الله أكبر ، الله أكبر ، الله أكبر
لا إله إلا الله والله أكبر ، الله أكبر ولله الحمد»

Allah is Great, Allah is Great, Allah is Great, Allah is Great. There is no deity save Allah and Allah is Great. Allah is Great. Praise be to Allah.

These words end the prayer.[147]

The preacher then climbs up to the pulpit to deliver the festival sermon. This should be a serious address concerning the meaning of the Feast and should deal with how Muslims should be loyal and sincere towards each other during the Feast, showing forbearance, exchanging visits, and giving assistance to each other. It should deal with piety, the performance of good deeds, obedience to the All-Merciful and All-Compassionate, and the renunciation of discord, hypocrisy, inequity, and disobedience. Its message should encompass all the sublime ideals expressed by Islam, the entrusting of the realization of these ideals to Muslims, and their Islamic adherence to values.

At the end of the sermon the preacher comes down from the pulpit and shakes hands with the congregation and everyone exchanges greetings and expressions of joy.

The prayer of the feast of sacrifice (*Id al-Adha*)

The prayer of the Feast of Sacrifice is exactly the same as that of the *Id al-Fitr*. The only difference is in the Resolve; in one you resolve to perform the Prayer of the Feast of the Breaking of the Fast, in the other you resolve to perform the Prayer of the Feast of Sacrifice.

In the Feast of the Breaking of the Fast there is no need[148] to say the Words of Greatness from the time of leaving one's house for the mosque, but in the Feast of Sacrifice, it is required by Tradition that you say them from the time of leaving your house until your arrival at the mosque.

The distinguished *imams* are all in agreement with what I have set down here regarding the prayers for the two feasts. They differ only as to the exact number of times the "Words of Greatness" should be recited, there being inconsistencies in the relevant evidence. The pattern most widely known and for which the evidence is strongest—and the opinion held by most *imams*—is as specified above, that is, seven times in the first *rak'ah* and five times in the second.

This may be compared with the ritual practised by the Hanafis, who say the "Words of Greatness" four times, plus once before the recitation in the first *rak'ah* and three times in the second *rak'ah* after the Opening Verse and the selected chapter of the Qur'an have come to an end. They say the Words of Greatness along with the bow. Every time they say the words during the two feasts, the *imam* and the worshippers raise their hands. Both methods are correct, being based upon evidence.

THE FUNERAL PRAYER (JANAZA)

Islam respects a Muslim, be he alive or dead. When a Muslim dies, our religion commands us to bathe him, perfume him, wrap him in a shroud, pray over him, take him to his final resting place, bury him, and invoke a blessing over him.

The prayer for the dead is a collective obligation. If it is performed by some, the others will be absolved of sin. It is a mercy and an honour for the dead person, and takes the following form. The deceased is laid pointing towards the Ka'bah. The *imam* stands at the head and shoulders of the deceased, if a man, and at the waist if it is the funeral of a woman. The worshippers stand to the right, to the left and behind him. The *imam* says the "Words of Greatness" four times and raises his hands on each occasion. The worshippers say them with him.

SAVE US FROM DOOM

Lord, I seek refuge in You from the promptings of the devils. Lord, I seek refuge in You from their presence.
(*Surah al-Mu'minum*, The Believers, 23:98-99).

Lord, we believe in You. Forgive us and have mercy on us; You are the Most Merciful.
(*Surah al-Mu'minum*, The Believers, 23:109).

Lord, ward off from us the punishment of Hell, for its punishment is everlasting.
(*Surah al-Furqan*, The Criterion, 25:65).

The first words of greatness

The *Imam* and the congregation recite, to themselves, the personal prayer of the Opening and Facing Allah,[149]

«سُبْحَانَكَ اَللّهُمَّ وَبِحَمْدِكَ ، وَتَبَارَكَ اسْمُكَ ، وَتَعَالَى جَدَّكَ وَلَا إِلٰهَ غَيْرُكَ» .

the Opening Verse (*al-Fatiha*) and some other verses.

REMEMBERING DEATH

Man has endless words at his disposal in this world; but there will come a time when he will be at a loss for words. There will be no one to listen to what he has to say, no press to print what he writes, and no loudspeaker to announce his words. The fool's paradise which he had constructed for himself in the world will have been razed to the ground. He will look for some respite from anguish and despair, but there will be none.

If only man were to remember death, the things which make him cruel and unjust would become meaningless; he would realize that his actions are leading him towards Hell. Man cannot make use of the wealth which he holds so dear before death comes and severs him from his earnings for all time. If man were to remember this fact, he would not be so obsessed with self-enrichment in this world. People plot the destruction of others, but before they can carry out their plots, death comes between them and their enemies. If one constantly keeps this fact in mind, one will never seek to harm others; one will never plot the downfall of another.

No one is ready to buy a house which is due to be demolished the next day. No one inhabits a city which is about to be devastated by an earthquake. Yet everyone makes the much more serious mistake of ignoring the most severe earthquake which will strike us—death.

— *Introducing Islam* by Maulana Wahiduddin Khan

The second words of greatness

The worshippers recite the "Words of Abraham" which are contained in the last "Words of Witness" of the "Words of Greeting." They are:

«اللهُمَّ صلِّ على مُحمَّدٍ وعلى آلِ مُحمَّدٍ كما صلَّيْتَ على إبْراهيمَ وعلى آلِ إبْراهيمَ ، وبارِكْ على مُحمَّدٍ وعلى آلِ مُحمَّدٍ كما بارَكْتَ على إبْراهيمَ وعلى آلِ إبْراهيمَ في العالَمـينَ إنَّكَ حميدٌ مجيدٌ».

O Lord, bless Muhammad and his family as You blessed Abraham and his family. Give Your blessing to Muhammad and his family as you gave Your blessing to Abraham and his family in the two worlds. You are the most praised, the most wonderful.[150]

The third words of greatness

Each one says this personal prayer separately:

«اللّهُمَّ اغْفِرْ لِحَيِّنا وَمَيِّتِنا ، وَشاهِدِنا وَغائِبِنا وَصَغيرِنا وَكَبيرِنا ، وَذَكَرِنا وَأُنْثانا ، اللّهُمَّ مَنْ أَحْيَيْتَهُ مِنّا فَأَحْيِهِ عَلَى الإِسْــلامِ وَمَنْ تَوَفَّيْتَهُ فَتَوَفَّهُ عَلَى الإِيمانِ».

O Lord, forgive us who are alive and those who are dead, we who are present and those who are absent, our young and our old, our men and our women. O Lord, he among us to whom you have brought to life, let him live as a Muslim. He whom You have caused to die, let him die in the Faith.[151]

The fourth words of greatness

This traditional personal prayer is said:

«اللّهُمَّ لا تَحْرِمْنا أَجْرَهُ وَلا تَفْتِنّا بَعْدَهُ ، وَاغْفِرْ لَنا وَلَهُ».

O Lord, do not deny us the reward which is his. Do not expose us to temptation after his death. Forgive us and forgive him.[152]

The *Imam* concludes the funeral prayers with the "Words of Peace," moving his head from right to left, saying:

السَّلامُ عَلَيْكُمْ وَرَحْمَةُ الله

May the Peace and the Mercy of Allah be upon you.

After the prayers, the deceased is carried to his final resting place, escorted with dignity, respect and personal prayer. At his final resting place it is required by tradition that those at the funeral should repeat the personal prayer for the dead, asking on behalf of the deceased for Allah's forgiveness, mercy, pleasure, and steadfastness when, bereft of all support, he is questioned by the two angels about his Lord, his religion, and his Prophet.

At funerals, the Prophet would say:

"Seek forgiveness for your brother and ask for steadfastness for him, for he is being questioned."[153]

At this time we also ask Allah to inspire us to give the correct answer when we are put to the proof, for all must taste death. We ask Allah to have compassion for us in our exile in this world and at the time of our death, in the loneliness of the grave, and when we stand before Him. We

STRENGTHEN US!

Lord, grant me a goodly entrance and a goodly exit, and sustain me with Your power.

(*Surah al-Isra'*, The Night Journey, 17:80).

ask Him to make easy for us the agony of death. He is All-Forgiving, All-Merciful.

THE PRAYER FOR ALLAH'S GUIDANCE (ISTIKHARA)

In all his affairs the Muslim seeks the help or power of his Exalted Lord. If something should happen to him, he takes refuge in prayer in which his soul is comforted and his anxieties eased. If he must make an important decision, he turns to prayer to seek Allah's guidance. If Allah guides him to action, he goes forward with it, being unconcerned with the outcome, for Allah is with him. But if Allah guides him to abandon his project for another, he thinks no more about it.

The prayer for Allah's Guidance is one of Allah's blessings. In it the worshipper faces his Lord, seeking His guidance and asking Him for whatever would be to his advantage, for whatever Allah would choose for him, and whatever would be in his best interest.

It is a matter of Tradition that the Prophet customarily taught his Companions the personal Prayer for Guidance, just as he taught them the verses of the Qur'an. If a Muslim is preparing to embark on an important task, he should pray about it and ask the guidance of his Lord. He should do as his Lord directs him, whether it means following or abandoning his course of action. The proper manner in which to perform the Prayer for Guidance is to recite two *rak'ahs* in addition to the obligatory duties and then, at the end of the prayer, to recite the "Words of Peace," followed by the personal prayer for guidance. Finally, one states what he desires, and then searches his heart. If the answer is favourable to the matter in hand, he should proceed with it; however, if the answer is that he should abandon it, he should do so. A Muslim never gives up something for Allah without its being replaced with something better. Here is the Tradition of the Messenger of Allah in which he instructs us in the Prayer for Allah's Guidance:

قال عليه الصلاة والسلام : «إذا همَّ أحدُكم بالأمر فليركعْ ركعتينِ مِنْ غيرِ الفريضة» ثُمَّ لِيقُلْ : اللهُمَّ إني أستخيرُك بعلمك وأستقدرُك بقدرتك وأسألُك من فضلك العظيم ، فإنَّك تقدرُ ولا أقدرُ ، وتعلمُ ولا أعلمُ ، وأنتَ علامُ الغيوب اللهُمَّ إنْ كُنتَ تعلمُ أنَّ هذا الأمرَ (ويُسَمِّي الأمرَ الذي همَّ بفعْله) خيرٌ لي في ديني ومعاشي وعاقبة أمري، ـ أو قال : عاجلِ أمري وآجله ـ فاقْدُرْه لي ، ويسِّرْهُ لي ، ثُمَّ باركْ لي فيه ، وإنْ كُنتَ تعلمُ أنَّ هذا الأمرَ (ويُسَمِّيه أيضًا) شرٌّ لي في ديني ومعاشي ، وعاقبة أمري . ـ أوْ قال : عاجلِ أمري وآجله ـ فاصرفْهُ عني واصرفْني عنهُ، واقْدُرْ لي الخيرَ حيثُ كانَ ثُمَّ أرضني به» .

If any one of you is concerned about a matter of importance, let him perform two rak'ahs other than the obligatory ones.

Then let him say: 'O Lord, I seek Your guidance, Your knowledge; I ask You to decide for Your glorious favour, for You decree and I do not. You know and I do not. You are He who knows the invisible.

O Lord, You know that this matter (and here he states the matter which concerns him) is of benefit to me in my religion, in my livelihood and in its outcome. Decide it for me and make it easy for me; then bless me in it (Or he says, 'Hasten the matter and its outcome.') And If You know that this matter (and here he names it again) is bad for me in my religion, in my livelihood, and in its outcome, turn it from me and divert me from it. Decree good for me wherever it may be, and make me pleased with it.[154]

THE PRAYER FOR THE ECLIPSE OF THE MOON AND THE SUN

Islam has given us a fine sense of propriety. It has taught us to take refuge in Allah whenever we find ourselves in adversity. We worship Him and we ask Him for help and assistance. We rely on Him and leave Him to decide what shall be done and how it shall be done. The eclipses of the moon and the sun are two natural phenomena which frequently cause dismay and unrest in those who witness them. For this reason it is the tradition of Islam to perform a special prayer relating to these phenomena to which the faithful resort in order to confide in their Lord. They recite from His Book, and through these prayers and through confiding in Allah, calm their souls. Afterwards they listen to the sermon in which the preacher speaks of the lesson to be learned from these manifestations. He draws the attention of the unmindful to the greatness of the Creator and how He is unrestricted in the universe; how He has the power to act in any way He wishes. "The sun and the moon are some of his signs." He does not have to answer for what He does, but they do.

The reason for the prayers in Connection with the Eclipse

The prayer in connection with the solar eclipse was prescribed during the last years of the Hijra. At that time Ibrahim, the beloved son of the Prophet died. On the very same day there was an eclipse of the sun and some people said that the sun had been eclipsed because of the death of Ibrahim.

This rumour spread until it came to the ears of the Prophet, who moved promptly to suppress the heresy and to explain the truth of such a disconcerting matter. Here is a *hadith* of *al-Bukhari* and *Muslim* narrated by Al-Mughira:

"There was an eclipse of the sun during the time of the Messenger of Allah on the day that Ibrahim died. The people said, 'The sun has been eclipsed because of the death of Ibrahim.' The Prophet said, 'The sun and the moon are two of Almighty Allah's signs and are eclipsed neither because of the death of anyone, nor for his being alive. If you see an eclipse, make a personal prayer to Almighty Allah and perform the prayer until it has passed."[155]

PRAYERS

Praise be to Allah, Lord of Creation, the Beneficent, the Merciful, King of Judgement Day. You alone we worship, and to You alone we pray for help. Guide us to the straight path, the path of those whom You have favoured, not of those who have incurred Your wrath, nor of those who have gone astray.

(Surah al-Fatihah, The Opening, 1:1-7).

How to perform the prayer of the Eclipse

The prayers of the eclipse respectively of the moon and the sun differ in form from the other prayers. They consist of two *rak'ahs* which are, preferably, performed in congregation, although the worshipper is permitted to perform his prayer alone. When they are performed in congregation, the *Imam* makes his recitations aloud and, at the end of the prayers, preaches a short sermon in which he speaks of the lesson to be learned from situations of this nature.

The prayer begins with the "Words of Greatness," then the recitation of the Opening Verse, followed by a recitation of an uncomplicated and preferably long passage from the Qur'an. This is followed by a bow, after which he stands erect and continues with the recitation, before the prostration. After this further recitation, each *rak'ah* consist of two bows and two prostrations and this he does in both the first and second *rak'ahs*.

Here is the tradition of 'A'isha. It is one of the genuine Traditions on which both *al-Bukhari* and *Muslim* are agreed. 'A'isha said:

"There was an eclipse of the sun during the lifetime of the Prophet. He went to the mosque where he stood and said the "Words of Greatness." He set the people in rows behind him and made a long recitation. Then he said the "Words of Greatness" and made a long bow which was shorter in duration than the first recitation. Then he raised his head and said, 'May Allah hear whoever praises Him. O Lord, Yours is the praise.' Then he stood up and made a recitation which was shorter than the first. Then he said the "Words of Greatness" and made a bow which was less than the first bow. Then he said, 'May Allah hear whoever praises him. O Lord, Yours is the praise.' Then he prostrated himself. Then he performed the other *rak'ah* in the same way until he had completed four bows and four prostrations. The sun had become visible again before he was finished. He then stood up and preached to the people, praising Allah for what He had made to appear and saying, 'the sun and moon are two of Almighty Allah's signs which are not eclipsed for the

death of anyone, nor for his being alive. If you see either one of them, hasten to prayer."[156]

Malik, Al-Shafi'i, Ahmad, and a whole host of scholars hold the opinion that the congregational prayer is a traditional requirement for the Prayer of the Eclipse, while Abu Yusuf and Muhammad say that a congregation is optional. The Iraqis, among whom is Abu Hanifa, say that it is a prayer to be performed alone. It is related in *Al-Bahr* (from *Al- 'Itra*) that both methods are correct.

Charity and forgiveness

May Allah reward Prophet Muhammad. May Allah's blessing and peace be upon him, he let no opportunity pass to further and promote the interests of his community, to show its members how to do good, and to beseech Allah's favour for his people. On the occasion of the eclipse of the moon or the sun, the Prophet urged his community to give alms, to remember Allah, to seek forgiveness, and to say the "Words of Greatness" during this strange phenomenon, which is but one of Allah's signs.[157]

A genuine Tradition relates that the Prophet said:

"The sun and the moon are two of Almighty Allah's signs and are eclipsed neither for the death of anyone, nor for his being alive."[158]

Conclusion

To conclude this book I ask Allah that He make it of benefit to people and that it be given to them without expectation of reward for myself in this life. In writing it, my aim was to serve my religion. There is no success except in Allah: in Him I place my trust and to Him I turn in repentance.

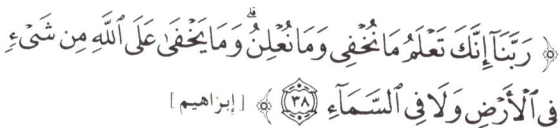

O Lord, You know what we do in secret and what we do openly. Nothing in Heaven or Earth can be hidden from Allah.

﴿ رَبِّ اجْعَلْنِي مُقِيمَ الصَّلَوٰةِ وَمِن ذُرِّيَّتِي ۚ رَبَّنَا وَتَقَبَّلْ دُعَاءِ ۝ رَبَّنَا اغْفِرْ لِي وَلِوَٰلِدَيَّ وَلِلْمُؤْمِنِينَ يَوْمَ يَقُومُ الْحِسَابُ ۝ ﴾ [إبراهيم]

O Lord, make me and my descendants dutiful in prayer. O Lord, accept this prayer. O Lord, forgive me my sins and those of my parents and all the faithful on the Day of Reckoning.

(*Surah Ibrahim,* Abraham, 14:40-41)

Praise be to Allah
May Allah Bless the Messenger and
Grant Salvation to him,
to his family, to his Companions,
and to whoever invokes Him in prayer
until the Day of Judgment.

Notes

1. Related by Tabarani in middle (2/1880) and others from Anas ibn Malik. See Shaikh Elalbany's book, *Saheiha* (No: 1358).
2. Related by al-Bukhari (No. 528) and Muslim (No. 667)
3. Related by Al-Tirmidhi (No. 2616), Al-Nasa'i (No. 414) in his book *Al-Tafseer*.
4. Related by Imam Ahmad (3/389) and Muslim (No. 82) from Jabir Ibn. Abd Allah.
5. Related by Imam Ahmad (5/346), Tirmidhi (no. 2621) Nasa'i (1/231), Ibn Maja (No. 1079) and others.
6. Related by Imam Ahmad (2/169), Abd Ibn Humayd (No.353) and others.
7. According to ibn Rushd, *Bidayt Al-Mujtahid* (1/90)
8. Related by Imam Ahmcd (3/389) and Muslim (No. 82) from Jabir Ibn. Abd Allah.
9. This is erroneous and should read: Related by Ibn al Naggar and Dailamy and notice that the rendering of transmission is very weak. For further information please see Al-Albani in his book *Al-Da'ifa* (No. 1098)
10. Related by Ibn Ab Hatim and Al-Tabarani in large from Ibn Abbas, see: *Al-D'aifa* (No: 2)
11. Related by Al-Tabarani in middle and the rendering of transmission is very weak, see Majma'a (1/302), (2/122)
12. Related by El-Bazzar (No. 348) and Ibn Hibban in *Maghruhin* (2/31) from Ibn Abas. The rendering of transmission is very weak, see *Al-Da'ifa* (No. 950), *Majma'a Al-Zawyed* (2/147),
13. The Arabic verb used here is the same as the verb "to pray". This section of the book is intended to clarify an apparent paradox in the Arabic language as related to Islamic teaching.

14. The argument is still primarily addressed to the Jews, but is of universal application, as in all the teachings of the Qur'an. The chief feature of Jewish worship was and still is the bowing of the head.

15. Related by Muslim (No.223) from Abu Malik El 'Ashari.

16. Related by Abu Da'ud (No. 61), Tirmidhi (No. 3), Ibn Maja (No. 275), Imam Ahamad (1/123, 129) and others, all from 'Ali Ibn Abi Talib. Also the Tradition related by Tirmidhi (No. 238), Ibn Maja (No. 276) Abu Ya'la (Nos. 1077, 1125) and others, from Abu Sa'id al-Khudari.

17. See Al-Albani in his book, *Ghayat Al-Maram* (No.71,72,113)

18. The Arabic word *siwak* means a small stick (the tip of which is softened by chewing or beating) used for cleaning and polishing the teeth.

19. Related by Al-Bukhari (Nos. 887, 7240) and Muslim (No. 252) from Abu Hurayra.

20. Related by Muslim (No. 234) from Umar.

21. Related by Al-Tirmidhi (No. 55)

22. Related by Al-Bukhari (No. 182) and Muslim (No. 272). See also Al-Arwa'a (Nos. 96, 97, 99. 100)

23. Related by Muslim (No. 343).

24. Also you can wash the legs in the ritual ablution, then pour the water liberally over the body.

25. Related by Al-Bukhari (Nos. 553,594) from Burayda.

26. The middle prayer (*Salat al wusta*) may be translated " the best or most excellent prayer". Authorities differ as to the exact meaning of this phrase. Most authorities seem to be in favour of interpreting this as the 'Asr prayer (in the middle of the afternoon). This is apt to be most neglected, and yet this is the most necessary, to remind us of Allah in the midst of our worldly affairs.

27. This is in Muslim countries. In non-Muslim countries consult your prayer timetable.

28. The Hijra denotes the date of the Prophet's migration from Makkah to Madina and the start of the Muslim era by which the Muslim calendar is now reckoned.
i.e., "A.H." means "after the Hijra".

[29] It is not related by Al-Bhukhari, but by Muslim (No. 385) from Umar.

[30] (No. 384).

[31] Related by Al-Bukhari (Nos. 614, 4719) from Jabir.

[32] This part is not from authentic tradition. See Alerwa'a (No. 243).

[33] Related by Al-Hakim (1/203-204) and Al-Bayhaqui (1/408), (3/131).

[34] This part is related by Abu Da'ud (No. 528), Bayhaqui (1/411) and others, but it is not an authentic tradition, because the rendering of transmission is weak. So we said: "The prayer is to be performed." Instead of "May Allah raise it up and make it last for ever."

[35] Related by Al-Bukhari (No. 403...) and Muslim (No. 526) and others.

[36] Jerusalem

[37] Related by Al Bukhari (No. 72288) and Muslim (No. 1337) from Abu Huraira.

[38] Related by Al Bhukhari (No. 4335 - terminates at No. 942)

[39] Related by Ahmad (2/20, 41), Muslim (No. 700) and Al-Tirmidhi (No. 2958) from Ibn Umar.

[40] Related by Al-Bukhari (No. 400) Muslim, and others from Jabir B. Abdullah.

- Also, related by Al-Bukhari (no. 1097 - Terminates at No. 1093), Muslim (no. 701), and others from Amir B. Rabi'a.

- Also, related by Muslim (No. 700) from Ibn Umar.

[41] The first chapter of the Quran

[42] Related by Muslim (No. 399R) from 'Umar. See Al-Erwa'a (No. 340, 341).

[43] Related by Bukahri (No. 744) and Muslim (No. 598) from Abu Hurayra.

[44] Related by Muslim (No. 771) from 'Ali ibn Abi Talib.

[45] This is an incorrect view. The correct procedure is to use it as the opening prayer each time the prayer is performed.

[46] Related by Muslim (No. 771). Abu Daud (no. 760), Tirmidhi (No. 3421, 3423), Nasa'I (2/129/No. 897), Ahmad (1/94, 95, 102 103) and others from Ali B. Abi Talib.

47 You can also recite long chapters. Please see *Sifat al-Salah* (pp. 83-98).

48 It is preferable that the worshipper raises his hands on four occasions: first, when saying the opening "Allah is Great", second when bowing, third when he stands upright after bowing, fourth when he stands up for the third rak'a.

- Al-Bayhaqi, relating from Al-Hakim says: "We know of no traditional law on which there was more agreement between the four caliphs, the ten who were promised paradise, and the Companions who came after him, as to its having emanated from the Prophet."

49 Related by Al-Bukhari (No. 799) from Refa'a B. Rafe'a.

50 Related by Muslim (No. 771) from Ali ibn Abi Talib.

51 Or more, as you like.

52 Related by Muslim (No. 482), Abu Dau'd (No. 875), Ahmad (2/421) and others from Abu Hurayra.

53 Related by Muslim (No. 771) from 'Ali.

54 Related by Ahmad (6/209) from 'A'isha. But the rendering of transmission is weak. Related by Muslim (No.2722) without determination the case time of prayer.

55 Related by Muslim (No. 486) and others from 'A'ishah.

56 Related by Al-Bukhari (No. 6398, 6399) and Muslim (No. 2719) from Abu Musa Al-Ash'ari.

57 Related by Abu Da'ud (No. 850), Al-Tirmidhi (No. 284, 285), Ibn Maja (No. 898) and others from Ibn Abbas. Please see Al-Erwa'a (No. 335)

58 This Arabic word is retained since the English language contain no equivalent for the complete ritual of one bow and two prostrations.

59 Related by Al-Bukhari (No. 6312) from Hudhaifa. And related by Muslim (No. 2711) from Al-Bara'a ibn. 'Azib.

60 Related by Muslim (No. 725) from 'A'isha.

61 See note 58

62 At this point the forefinger of the right hand is raised in a slight movement, a symbolic indication of the Oneness of Allah.

[63] Related by Al-Bukhari (No. 831) and Muslim (No. 402) from Abd Allah ibn. Mas'ud.

[64] Related by Muslim (No. 405) from Aby Mas'ud Al-Ansary. Also Related by Al-Bakhari (No. 3370) from Ka'ab B. Ogra See *Sefat Al-Salah* (pp. 164-172).

[65] Related by Muslim (No. 771) from 'Ali.

[66] Related by Al-Bukhari (No. 834) and Muslim (No. 2705).

[67] Related by Al-Bukhari (Nos. 2823, 4707) and Muslim (No. 2706) from Anas. The tradition is a general one (inside the prayer and outside it).

[68] Related by Muslim (No. 591) from Tawban.

[69] Related by Ahmad (4/227); the rendering of transmission is weak.

[70] Related by Al-Bukhari (No. 844), Muslim (No. 593) and others.

[71] See Nasa'i in his book, *Amal Alyum w'Allila*(No. 100), Ibn Alsunni (No. 124), Tabarani (No. 7532) and others. Also see Al Albani in his book *Al-Saheha* (No. 972).

[72] Related by Abu-Tabarani (No. 2733).

[73] Related by Abu Da'ud (No. 1523), Al-Tirmidhi (No.2903), Al Nasa'i (3/68/ No. 1336), Ahmed (4/155, 201) and others from Uquba.

[74] Related by Abu Dau'd (No. 5079, 5080), Ahmad (4/234), Ibn Hibban (No. 2346 - *Mawarid*) and others with a weak rendering of transmission.

[75] It is not to be found in the last Tradition.

[76] Related by Muslim (No. 597) from Abu Hurayra.

[77] Also anyone can say the Words of Glory thirty-three times, then the Words of Praise thirty three times, then the Words of Greatness thirty-three times.

[78] See note 62.

[79] Related by Muslim (No. 710) from Abu Hurayrah.

[80] Related by Abu Da'ud (No 1272), Al-Tirmidhi (No. 430), Ahmad (2/117) and others from Abd Allah B. Umar.

[81] Related by AI-Bukhari (No. 624), Muslim (No. 838) and others from Abd Allah ibn Mughaffal.

[82] Surah, 88.

[83] Surah, 109.

[84] Surahs, 112-114.

[85] Related by Ibn Hebban (No. 680 - *Mawared*) and others from Abu Huraira.

[86] Related by Ibn Khudhiyma (No. 1100), Ibn Abi Shayba (2/314, 315), (10/387, 388, 389), Abdul Razaq (No. 4968, 4969), Al-Bayhaqi (2/210, 211) and others from Umar, his saying.

[87] Related by Abu Da'ud (No. 1425), Tirmidhi (N. 464), Al-Nasa'I (3/248/ Nos. 1745, 1746), Ibn Maja (No. 1178), Ahmad (1/199, 200/Nos. 1718, 1723, 1727) and others from Al-Hasan B. Ali.

[88] Related by Abu Da'ud (No. 652), Ibn Hebban (No. 357-*Mawrid*), Tabarani (Nos. 7164m 7165, Al-Hakim (1/260), Al-Bayhaqi (2/432) and others from Shadad B. Aws.

[89] Related by Al-Bukhari (No. 853) and Muslim (No. 561) from Ibn Umar.

- Also related by Al-Bukhari (No. 854) and Muslim (No. 564) from Gaber.

- Also related by Al-Bukhari (No. 856) and Muslim (No. 562) from Anas ibn Malik.

[90] Good without mention of forgiveness. Related by Tirmidhi (No. 314), Ibn Maja (No. 771), Ahmad (6/282, 283) and others from Fatimah.

- This meaning also related by Muslim (No. 713) from Abu Hymayd or Abu Usa'id.

[91] Related by Al-Hakim (1/218) and Al-Bayhaqui (2/442) from Anas. Also Al-Bukhari (1/523) relates by suspension from Ibn Umar that he steps inside the mosque with the right foot first and when he leaves the mosque he steps outside with the left foot first.

[92] Related by Abu Da'ud (No. 921) Al-Tirmidhi (No. 390), Al-Nasa'I (3/10), Maja (No. 1245), Ahmad (2/233, 248, 284, 473, 475, 490) and others from Abu Huaira.

[93] Related by Al-Bakhari (No. 516) and Muslim (No. 543) from Abi qutada.

[94] Related by Abu Da'ud (No. 922), Al-Nasa'I (3/11/No.1205), al-Tirmidhi (No.601), Ahmad (6/31,183,234), Abu Ya'la (No.4406), Ibn Hebban (No. 2355 - A1Ehsan) and others from Ai'sha with a good rendering of transmission.

[95] The Tradition in the line is an incorrect one, please see Al-Abbani in his book, *Tamam Al-Minna* (pp.300-302).

[96] Related by Al-Bukhari (No. 509) and Muslim (No. 505) from Abi Sa'id Al-Khudri.

- Also related by Muslim (No. 506) from Ibn Umar.

[97] Related by Al-Bukhari (No.797) and Muslim (No.676) from Abu Hurayra.

- Also Related by Al-Bukhari (No.1002) and Muslim (No.677) from Anas. Also see Sah'in Ibn Khodhaima (No.619,620).

[98] Related by Muslim (No. 772) from Huzaifa.

[99] Related by Abu Da'ud (No. 884).

[100] Related by Muslim (No.540) from Jabir.

- Also related by Ahmad (2/10) and Ibn Khudhaima (No.888) from Ibn Umar.

[101] Related by Al-Bukhari (No.829) and Muslim (No.570) from Abd Allah Ibn Buhaina.

- Also related by Muslim (No. 571) from Abi Sa'id Al-Khudri and (No.574) from Emran Ibn Al-Hosa'in.

[102] Related by Al-Bukhari (No.482) and Muslim (No.573) from Abi Huraira.

- Also related by Al-Bukhari (No.401) and Muslim (No 572) from Abd Allah Ibn Mas'oud.

[103] Related by Al-Bukhari (No. 1117) from Emran.

[104] Related by Al-Darqutni (2/42-43) from Aly. See Erwa'a Al-Ghalil (No.558).

[105] Related by Al-Bukhari (No. 645) and Muslim (No. 650)

[106] Related by Abu Da'ud (No.547), Al-Nasa'i (2/106-107/ No.847), Ahmed (5/196), (6/446), and others.

107 Related by Ahmad (3/439) and Al-Tabarani (20/ Nos. 394, 395) with a weak rendering of transmission.

108 Related by Abu Da'ud (No. 552), Ibn Maja (No.792) Ahmad (3/423), Ibn Khodhaima (No. 1480), Al-Hakim (1/247), Al-Bayhaqi (3/58), and Al-Baghawi (No.796) with a good rendering of transmission.

- Muslim (No. 653), from Aby Hurayrah.

109 Related by Ahmed (3/367), Abu Ya'la (No. 1803), Ibn Hebban (No. 428 - Mawared) and Tabarani in the Middle from Jabir Ibn Abd Allah, with a weak rendering of transmission.

110 Related by Abu Da'ud (No. 567), Ahmed (2/76, 77) and others from Ibn Mas'ud.

111 Related by Muslim (No. 673) from Aby Mas'ud Al-Ansary.

112 Related by Al-Bukhari (No. 723) and Muslim (No. 433) from Anas.

- Also related by Al-Bukhari (No. 722) and Muslim (No. 435) from Abu Huraira.

- Also related by Ahmad (3/322), Abu Ya'la (No. 2168) and Al-Tabarani (No. 1744) from Jabir.

113 This is not good and correct view, because the chain of authorities (*isnad*) which goes right back to the source of the Tradition is very weak.

- Please see Al-Da'efa (Nos. 921,922), Al-Erw'a (No. 541) and Tamam Al-Minna (pp. 285,286).

114 Very weak. Related by Al-Darqutni (2/87-88) and Al-Bayhaqi (3/90) from Ibn Umar, with a very weak rendering of transmission. Please see Al-Da'efa (No. 1822).

115 Related by Al-Tabarani (No. 777), Al-Darqutni (2/88), Al-Hakim (3/222) and others from Marthad Ibn Abi Marthd. Al-Ghanwy, with a weak rendering of transmission. See Al-Da'efa (No.1823).

116 Related by Al-Bukhari (No. 350) and Muslim (No. 685) from 'Ai'sha.

- Also related by Muslim (No. 687) from Ibn Abbas.

117 Related by Al-Bazzar (No. 990), Ibn Hibban (No. 913-*Mawarid*), Al-Tabarani in the large (No. 11880,11881), Abu Nu'aim (6/276) and

others from Ibn Abbas. Please see Erw'a *Al-Jhalil* (No. 564).

[118] Related by Al-Bukhari (No. 1080) from Ibn 'Abbas.

[119] Not the modern measure. The mile referred to was equal to 4,000 cubits, or approximately 1250 or 1848 metres, depending on the country.

[120] A farasang is about 3.14 miles (modern measure).

[121] Related by Muslim (No.691).

[122] *Mauquf* (it is a Tradition going back only to a Companion). Related by Malik in *Al-Muwatta* (1/149), Abdul Razzaq (Nos. 4369, 4370 4371), Ibn Abi Shaybah (1/383) and others from Umar.

[123] The correct view, that is the second one. (That the traveller perform the prayer in full behind a resident).

[124] Related by Ahmed (1/216), Abu Awana (2/340), and others with a good rendering of transmission. Also see Muslim (No. 688), Al Nasa'i (3/199 Nos.1443,1444), Ahmad (1/226,290,337,369) and others.

[125] Related by Muslim (No. 694).

[126] Related by Ahmed (5/241,242), Abu Da'ud (No.1220), Al-Tirmidhi (No.553), Ibn Hibban (Nos.1456,1589 Al-Ihsan), Al-Darqutni (1/392-393), Al-Hakim in Ma'rifa (pp.119-120), Al-Bayhaqui (3/163), Al-Baghawi in *Sharh Al-Sunna* (No. 1042) and others from Mu'adh. See Erwa'a Al Jhalil (No. 578).

[127] Related by Ahmad (1/367-368), Abdul Razzaq (No. 4405), Al Darqutni (1/388), Al-Bayhaqi (3/163, 164) and others from Ibn Abbas. Please see Al-Erwa'a (No.579).

[128] Related by Muslim (No. 652) from Ibn Mas'ud. Please see Faith Al-Bari (2/127,128).

[129] Please see Al-Erw'a (No.594).

[130] Related by Muslim (No. 865) from Ibn Umar and Abu Huraira.

[131] Related by Abu Da'ud (No. 1052), Al-Tirmidhi (No. 500), Al Nasa'i (3/88/ No. 1369), Ibn Maja (no. 1125), Ahmad (3/424, 425), Abu Ya'la (No. 1600) and others, from Abu Al-Ga'ed Al-Damury, with a good rendering of transmission. Please see *Sahih al-Targhib* (Nos. 726-734).

[132] Very weak. Related by Ibn Maja (No. 1081), Al-Uquaili (2/298), Abd Ibn Humaid (No. 1136), Abu Ya'la (No. 1856), Al-Bayhaqi (3/90, 171) and others from Jabir, with a very weak rendering of transmission.

[133] See page (No. 152).

[134] Related by Al-Bukhari (Nos. 444, 1163), Muslim (No. 714) from Abu Quatada.

[135] It is not established in the Traditions.

[136] Related by Al-Bukhari (No. 934) and Muslim (No. 851) from Abu Hurayra.

- Also related by Abu Da'ud (No. 347), Ibn Khosaima (No. 1810) and others from Ibn Amru, with a good rendering of transmission.

- Also related by Abu Da'ud (No. 1051) and Ahmad (1/93) from Ali Ibn Abi Talib.

[137] Related by Muslim (No.881) from Abu Hurairah.

[138] Related by Al-Bukhari (No. 937) and Muslim (No. 729, 882) from Ibn Umar.

[139] The tradition traced to the Prophet is very weak. But Al-Bayhaqi (3/278) relates it with a sound rendering of transmission from Ali (*Mawkuf*).

- Also related by Malik (1/177) and Al-Bayhaqi (3/2780 from Ibn Umar.

[140] Related by Al-Bukhari (No. 953) from Anas Ibn Malik

[141] No, but he says the Words of Greatness.

[142] It is recommended that the *Imam* explain how this prayer is performed before it starts, because being performed only twice a year, it may be that many people are not very sure how to perform it.

[143] See *Ma'rifat Al Sunan wa' Al-Athar* (5/67-75), Irwa'a Al-Jhalil (No.639), *Zad Al-Ma'ad* (1/443) and others.

[144] See Al-Erwa'a (No. 642) and Tamam Al-Minna (pp. 349-350).

[145] The Tradition related by Muslim (No. 878).

[146] The Tradition related by Muslim (No. 878).

[147] These words are not established in Traditions.

[148] No, the Words of Greatness are required by Tradition in both of the Feasts, The Feast of Breaking of the Fast and in the Feast of Sacrifice (Al-Adha and Al-Fitr).

[149] Please see note 42.

[150] See note 64.

[151] Related by Abu Da'ud (No. 3201), Al-Tirmidhi (No. 1024), Ibn Maja (No. 1498) and others from Abi Huraira. Please see *Ahkam Al-Ganayes* (p.124).

[152] Related by Abu da'usd (No. 3201), Ibn Maja (No. 1498) and others from Abi Huraira. The Tradition is authentic without the last words (Forgive us and forgive him). Please see *Ahkam Al-Janazas* (pp.123-125).

[153] Related by Abu Da'ud (No. 3321). Abd Allah Ibn Ahmad in the "Zuhd" (2/42). Ibn Al-Sunny (No. 585). Al-Hakim (1/370) Al-Bayhaqi (4/56) and others from Usman Ibn Affan, with a good rendering of transmission.

[154] Related by Al-Bukhari (No. 1162) from Jabir Ibn Abd Allah.

[155] Related by Al-Bukhari (No. 10430 and Muslim (No. 215).

[156] Related by Al-Bukhari (No. 1044) and Muslim (No. 901).

[157] Related by Al-Bukhari (No. 1044) and Muslim (No. 901) from 'A'isha.

[158] See note 155.